North t

Recollections of a Tribal Chief

Lynne Symonds (Luccock)

First published in 2018 by Tunstall Hill Ltd.

For Alison and Rachel
With my love as always
Mum xx

Contents

This memoir is formed of shards of memory, diary entries, and recollections of my childhood origins in Sunderland in the North of England, and my later, totally privileged involvement in Northern Ghana where I found surprising similarities.

I am a chemistry teacher and will clearly never be a writer as the reader will see! This an attempt to record some of the many unique experiences gained from working closely with impoverished and neglected communities who just needed a hand in their brave and often frustrated attempts to move from poverty.

Preface

The wonderful people of Northern Ghana love to party. It is awe inspiring to be part of all-consuming celebrations that can spring up spontaneously, with talking drums passing news between mud compounds and from village to village. Even in 2018, where many have mobile phones, the drums play their vital role in communication. The air will throb, dusts thicken, and crowds hurry to celebrate, wearing their finest cloths and smocks.

Late spring 2018 will see a glorious party to celebrate the 25th anniversary of the opening of Wulugu Senior High School – Wulugusec – by Kariumu Nachina. This is where it all began. In 1993 there were just forty students and five teachers, but so few girls that Karimu fought for a hostel for them. Now there are almost two thousand students. Over six thousand have graduated from the school, with numbers increasing each year. No mean achievement for Karimu, who, as a small boy was driven away from home because he was so clever.

In the extreme heat, I will see crowds from every mud hut hurrying towards the village; children running and dancing, old men leaning on the arms of others, women laughing and waving to us with welcoming smiles. I will, as I have done many times before, listen, watch, dance and celebrate with these joyous friends. After so many visits to this region, I would like to think that I have become accepted not just as a chief, or a representative of a charity, but an equal who shares with the people their hopes, problems, joys and values. Nevertheless, I will still be wondering how much more we could be doing.

Much later, exhausted, slowly heading back to Tamale to rest, I will think about the day, and the years, and the changes. In the UK I had become used to people asking me about our work, wanting to tell me about their donations to the better-known charities. I always praised them, becoming used to the fact that those who have much do not often share, while those with little help where they can.

Although I am honoured with Ghanaian Chieftaincies, and recognition from the UK, the most important things are the strong friendships in both places that are nothing to do with money, rather people trying to make lives better for others. Those who benefitted from what Karimu began are now to be found across Ghana and in many parts of the world. It is unlikely and unnecessary for them be aware of the work that this man from the Mamprusi tribe of the North of Ghana, together with a policeman's daughter from the North of England did to help so many out of poverty.

In keeping with Ghanaian beliefs about the after-life, Karimu will be partying along with everyone else at Wulugusec for this year's celebrations. His Chief, Neesim Poanaba will, as ever, be looking at her watch and wanting to move on.

Lynne Symonds Easter 2018

Chapter One
The Library

The books on the shelves stood aloof in the punishing heat of a Ghanaian afternoon. Dust rose from the parched earth outside, as the people of Wulugu celebrated the arrival of the books. The air was heavy with the sound of drumbeats spreading the news.

When the heat of the day relented, Karimu set out to walk the ten miles that would take him to the nearest telephone. He wanted to share the story of the celebrations of his village, and the hundreds of other villages that housed the people of his tribe, The Mamprusi people.

He called my number in a remote farmhouse in Norfolk, England. 'My friend, it is Karimu, we have done it,' he said. His mission complete, he stood a while, replaying the conversation in his mind, trying to make sure that he could recall every word, as he knew he would have to recount it many times the next day. He willed his feet, against all the instincts of the tiredness threatening to overwhelm him, to retrace their steps. As he walked, the big African moon shone down on the lone figure still trying to believe that it had actually happened. The events, which had brought the books to Karimu's village, began many years earlier, as does my own story.

***

On 18th August 1947, I was born to Mary and Tom Luccock whose own roots were embedded deep in the earth and culture of North East England. My home was to be an upstairs flat, with no running water and a shared toilet in the yard, but Mary and Tom brought me home with no sense of regret for the circumstances that others might have regarded as hardship. For them, life had never been better. They had survived the horrors of the Second World War, Tom had found secure employment in the police force, they had their own rented home, and now they had me.

As Mary lay sleeping, Tom held me in his arms looking up out of the window at a paler version of the constant moon that had looked over him during his times in the jungles of Burma. He rocked me gently and quietly, singing his lullaby.

'Too ra loo ra loo ra loo ra baby
Do you want the moon to play with or the stars to run away with, hush now don't you cry'

He knew that he had never felt happier in his life. 'Little one,' he whispered, 'this is a wonderful life and we are going to have so many adventures.'

***

Meanwhile 5000 miles away, Karimu's own story begins. He was born in a hut made of mud and straw thatch in a village called Lukula, in a large district called 'Over-seas'. An area so named because when the rain came it was cut off from the surrounding land for weeks or months. His parents were glad he was a boy, but there was the problem of how they would feed him until he had grown tall enough to be able to work and make a contribution to his survival. I wonder if the fates had already decreed that his own life was to become entwined with the small scrap of life that was being celebrated in Tom's arms.

Karimu tells his own story.

I, Karimu Nachina was born on Saturday 8ᵗʰ April 1946 in the village of Lukula, Northern Ghana. My father was Datia Nachina, and my mother Mumuna Tia, a widow with five other children. I was the third boy to be born, the first two dying as toddlers, even though they seemed strong and promising. This drew some envy from my father's other three wives and they took the collective decision that Mumuna could have her children from the previous marriage, but that no child in her new home could compete with their own children for the inheritance that would be left by my father. Besides, to keep adding boys to the first two from the earlier marriage would be too great a blessing for my mother. Those first two boys had to die, and they died.

When my mother was pregnant again soothsayers were consulted to know what sex I would be. Four were consulted and their findings unanimous: she would give birth to the same boy that kept coming back. Then there was a new revelation. A boy from Mumuna who would survive in the house would prosper and carry the Nachina name. In other words, I would survive all my other brothers and be the future landlord of the house. My mother was considered an intruder that had won the heart of their husband because she was a better cook. Another decision was made. Mumuna must die with the pregnancy. No chance was to be given for me to survive. My father's first son was already a father of four, who went to consult a soothsayer to know his future and that of his children. It was him who brought back the news of the secret conspiracy by my mother's rivals. Alarmed at the news, my father consulted three more seers who all confirmed that the conspirators had been at work for too long and had finished their plan, and that no amount of sacrifice could save the life of Mumuna and me, her unborn child. But as fate would have it, her ninth month of pregnancy was April, the beginning of the rainy season. The weather usually gets too hot and people sleep in the open compound for fresh air. On 8th April at about 10pm there was a rainstorm and people were hastily awakened to rush into their rooms. Mumuna barely got to her room when I came out and started yelling. My father, my brother Takora and Takora's son got together and wondered what had happened to reverse the plans of the 'evil ones.' Maybe God had his own plan?

Although I was born, the plan to eliminate me continued. One day, when I was just seven months old, my mother put me in the middle of the compound house to shit, while she waited nearby to clean me. There was a dog wanting to help her by eating the faeces. But in a flash, the dog gave a piercing cry. It had been taken by a leopard. Where it came from and how it got to the middle of the compound in broad daylight soothsayers had to explain. Their findings were linked to the pre-birth conspiracy. I was the target and should have been caught and eaten by the leopard. By a coincidence, I was being bathed by my mother in a walled bathroom between two rooms at around 5pm when the leopard attempted to scale the wall of our house. It slipped and fell back into a trap that had been set behind the wall. The leopard was killed that evening and people began to congratulate my mother. When she asked why, she was told that the leopard was an old lady turned into a leopard to catch me. The following morning an old lady died in the house.

My father grew sick and did not survive the farming season that year, and my mother was a widow once again. She moved with her children to her village four miles away to keep me safe. I was an oddball and no child wanted to play with me after being warned by their mothers to keep away from the boy that leopards could not eat. Against all the odds I survived, becoming tall and strong for such a young boy. I could work, hunt and solve problems better than all of my friends. Yet I knew that life was not guaranteed, that if the rains did not come in time there would be no food. I knew too much already about disease and death. I also understood that the people of my village suspected that I was a witch, as I knew too many things for a boy of my age.

Three hundred miles away, in the capital of Accra the government passed a decree that three male children from each village in the forgotten lands of the North should go to school. A white man came to my village to identify the three children. The children were to be produced by the first three elders of the village. My uncle Takora was now the village elder, followed by two others. The other two elders quickly named their children but my uncle had no child of school age. He looked up to his elder brother, but he refused to give up a child as he thought that anyone who went with the white man went straight to hell after death. My uncle had to find a child or be disgraced. Someone reminded him of me, his nephew living in Kpatarigu, and consulted my brothers on their return from the farm. My brothers would not even wait until the next morning. A horse rider was dispatched to Kpatarigu to get me. There was no horse in my mother's village so the horse was a big attraction. When I got the news that I was to ride a horse to my village I was very excited, but my mother and sisters were all wailing and did not continue the cooking that night. They slept hungry but I had a triumphant ride to my village. When asked whether I would go to school I said 'yes', not knowing what school was.

The school village was forty-six miles away. I was to stay there for five months of the school term and then had a vacation of one month back in the village. But, although I was tall, I was declared not grown enough to start school by the teacher. My brother who had carried me there - also an orphan - was happy to take me back home. The head teacher saw us and asked why we were leaving. My brother explained, but the head master knew that I wouldn't be brought back the following year if I left now. So I started school and was given to an old lady called Comfort, to take care of me.

***

I had no idea that we were poor. It was soon after the end of the war, and everyone was constrained by rationing. Any money worries that my parents had were kept hidden from me. The only world I knew was the warren of streets surrounding the small flat where we lived. There was no television, and few radio programmes, so we made our own entertainment in the boundless realms of childhood imagination. On weekends and summer evenings my friends and I played in the yards and lanes, and on the bombsites, creating imaginary castles and countries amongst the debris of demolition. On winter nights or days when the weather was harsh, my parents replaced friends as playmates. Life was very easy and uncomplicated then. I knew that I was the centre of my parents' world and that our cosy little flat was a fortress against anything bad. I was five years and three weeks old on the day I started school, walking the two hundred yards from our front door to the school gates, holding Tom's hand tight, trying not to let the feeling that was a mixture of fear and excitement take control. As he so often seemed to, Tom guessed what was

19

happening, 'don't worry poppet you'll be fine. Mam will be here to pick you up at dinner time and when we both get home at tea time you can tell us the stories of your day.' Days rolled into weeks and the rows of desks and predictable routines contained our boisterousness and encouraged our potential. It was here that I met my first hero, Mr Spencer, the first person outside of my family who was to have a lasting influence on my life. Outwardly there was nothing remarkable about Maurice Spencer, but, for me, he possessed the gift of being able to make learning exciting, to make education valuable. Many years later, standing on a dusty plain in Africa I found myself thinking about my first classroom in Chester Road Junior School, and of Margaret Ellis and Maurice Spencer, my inspirations to become a teacher. The idea that lovely, strict, Mrs Ellis would, over half a century later, help me to build a school in Africa, was beyond any dream.

***

Against all odds, Karimu survived. He could work and hunt and solve problems better than all his friends. But he knew that life was not safe, that there were many problems that could not be solved. He knew that if the rains did not come in time there would be no food. He knew about disease and death, but was only just beginning to understand that there were other ways in which life was not safe. The people of his village, who understood the ways of witchcraft, suspected that he himself must be a witch because he knew too many things for a boy of his age. Who knows what would have become of him had the fates not chosen this moment to intervene in his destiny when, three hundred miles away in the capital of Accra the government had passed a decree that three male children from each village in the forgotten lands of North Ghana should go to school. The elders of his village found their solution. Even though they were unsure of these new plans for education they were unsure of Karimu too, and so he was chosen to go to school in the larger community of Pigu.

Chapter Two
Tom

Tom's father, George senior, was a miner in Sacriston, a local Sunderland pit. His father before him had done the same, toiling in the heat and darkness hour after hour, but somehow able to overcome the horrors by joining the pit's brass band. He'd proudly polish his old trumpet, cleaning it almost as much as he did himself, afraid that dirt would damage its clarity of tone. George had been afraid of the dark, afraid of the dust and the heat ever since he was first sent down the pit shaft at thirteen, making him the butt of jokes from others who seemed stronger and tougher. He lived with his wife Elizabeth – 'Lizzie-Ann' they called her - in a cottage provided by the mine masters, one of the bribes needed to ensure that men would forfeit their health for their families. There were two bedrooms with thin walls, a scullery, and a kitchen with a cooking range. All life happened in the stuffy kitchen that was constantly damp from drying clothes. Baths were rare, yet after every one of George's shifts, Lizzie-Ann would carry in the water, heat it on the fire in large, dented pans and scrub at her husband's skin with her worn-out hands. Life was tough, but she found ways to make it bearable. Lizzie-Ann had three children; George, Jane and Tom. Tom was born a weakling, who they were sure would not survive. When he was four days old, the priest was brought to the house to baptise him. This was the first of many battles that Tom's body fought to stay alive. This time, as would often happen over the years, he recovered and started school when he was five. Brother George walked with him. Tom was a willing follower at first, enjoying many days off school as they ran around the markets, helping themselves to whatever wasn't closely guarded by the hawkers.

Jane, two years older, was more like young Tom, but somehow born without the fire that was needed to live this harsh life. Lizzie-Ann cared for her three children. She was a survivor, doing what was needed to make the best of times where food money had sometimes been spent on beer and cigarettes, and the pit coal allowance was sold to pay the rent. If Tom didn't have shoes, then he would have to stay at home. Yet first-born George always had shoes. Lizzie-Ann was a tall and attractive woman, with hair fashionably permed and the regulation housewife's overall pinched tight at the waist. Her clear blue eyes missed nothing, and her brain was keen and alert. Tom was puzzled one day, coming home early, unwell from his infant school. The back door, always open, was locked. He lay shivering on the floor of the squalid shared toilet across the yard, and was disturbed by whispered goodbyes, and the sight of Bob, a family friend, hurrying away in the shadows, at the same time as his dad, coughing and bent, carried his bait tin slowly up the street. Jane, meanwhile, was going through another of her increasingly frequent spells of sickness. Sickness was in the air, along with the fog and the coal dust. Jane, like many others, did not have the resistance to deal with the constant barrage of infection.

This time it must have been serious. The doctor was called. Doctors in those days did not call without payment. He was a large man with a balding head and highly coloured cheeks. He knew that most would have a painful, gasping death, families calling him in when all hope seemed lost, believing that he could perform the necessary magic. But Jack Shaw was a *Robin Hood*, happily over-charging his wealthy business clients, and undercharging the pit families. He gently pulled back the sheet and felt Jane's failing pulse. As she coughed, her breath rattled and her chest heaved.

Tom watched, very afraid for his sister, his young mind knowing that things were so very wrong, but yet again, not knowing what to do. It was the day of Jane's funeral when he began to realise just how lonely he was in that house. The family had a small mongrel, Meg, that lived in the coal shed. Meg was not allowed in the cottage as she was always dirty and howled a great deal. But she was quiet and content when Tom came to take her out to play. Tom loved Meg. He understood that Meg had to die, as she was thin and limping badly, yet he never understood the death of his sister. He also worried more than ever about his dad. How could he protect him from the terrible cough that never stopped? So, young Tom Luccock became stronger, his mind sharper. He grew closer to his dad, and soon the family seemed to be divided. George was his mother's favourite, and he always sided with her. Then there was Tom with his kind and caring dad, aware of his youngest son's vulnerability, and determined to help him find more joy in his life. Tom liked being at school, and his teachers liked him. He was interested in everything, and asked many questions. Not many of these pit children could understand figures, but young Tom could outwit some of the teachers with his quick mind. They talked in the staffroom about how much more he would learn if he attended more often. But he needed to work, and Uncle Jimmy had a stall at Durham market. Tom got up before dawn and walked the six miles to Durham town centre. If there was bread in the pantry he would pull off a hunk to eat on the way. If Lizzie-Ann had made flat cake, he took some for Uncle Jimmy as well. Jimmy paid him sixpence a day, and sometimes paid a penny for him to take the tramcar home if he was very tired. Jimmy, who had never been a miner, travelled to South Shields to buy from the ships in port, finding that the store-men were more than pleased to offload their damaged goods. He worked hard but made a better living than others, often finding that he needed an extra pair of hands. Tom was a remarkably polite boy, just like his dad and granddad before him. Customers loved him, feeling sorry for him in his ragged clothing, and this made them buy more. There were days when Tom had no shoes however, and couldn't manage the walk. On other days he had no jumper and on the wettest of days no coat. Jimmy made a bargain with Lizzie-Ann that she would let him know when Tom's shoes were too small, so that he could look out for something in time.

George senior was increasingly concerned for his younger son. George junior would be fine, he was already skilled at driving deals, scheming, getting what he wanted. But Tom was different. He was a tall, good-looking boy who was always polite and kind. But there would be nothing for him except the pit. His mother was already spending his pay in her mind. So, one biting December morning, he took Tom to the pithead. 'This is it bonny-lad. Time to look at where you will be doing your shifts.' As he pushed him forward, peering into the black nothingness, terror shot through Tom's body, his stomach making its first comment with a stab of pain. Pain that Tom would remember in the years ahead as it would take command of his life. 'No dad, I'm not brave like you and the rest, please can we go home?' And that was that. Tom had been a star attender at Chapel Sunday school. Reverend Peters was from London, and knew that Tom could never face a mining life, that he was meant for something different. But he couldn't understand why George hadn't been sent to London or down the pit. In fact, one thing that his mam and dad agreed on was that he would soon get into trouble in London. George and the coppers had already met several times. He had wanted to go to the pit, show that he was a man, but swearing at the gaffer on the second day had earned him the sack. After that, he decided to take the easy road. He did not want to be told what to do by anyone.

Tom was a bright boy, but there was no chance of any more learning in school. So it was all arranged. Fourteen-year-old Thomas Mann Luccock was off to London; the boy who had never travelled beyond Durham. Uncle Jimmy found him a brown case. One of the fasteners was broken, but the other was OK. His mam packed a hunk of ham and egg pie, which fitted between the socks and a new blue shirt that Jimmy had given him. 'Tom lad, this shirt hasn't sold on the market, it's taking up space I need, so can you find a use for it?' This was the first new thing that Tom had ever owned. Everything he wore was a hand-me-down, usually from brother George. George never cared about his clothes and so they were often torn with missing buttons when they reached Tom. This is how he first learned to sew. Many years later, Tom put this skill to good use helping his youngest, aspiring 'hippie' daughter create wild clothes for the seventies scene.

At Durham station noise roared around him. Handsome for his fourteen years, Tom was afraid. He wanted to hold his dad's rough hand and go home.

'Come on Lizzie-Ann, the boy needs a few shillings to tide him over. It's payday Friday, then he'll send it all back to you - and more,' said his dad, pleading in his gentle way.

'Where do you think I'd get money from?' she shrieked, her clear blue eyes shining with anger. Tom patted his trouser pocket, knowing that Dad had gone without his pint all week to help him on his way. How he loved this troubled miner. He noticed that his dad did not hear so well and that his cough was almost always there. Tom knew that all miners coughed, that listening to blasts underground had inevitable consequences for hearing. All Tom worried about was that his dad might die, be blown up, be suffocated and buried. Then the train arrived.

'Here it comes lad. Now hang onto your ticket,' he said. 'Missus, he said to a woman sitting in his carriage, 'ah'd be grateful if yer could keep an eye on my boy. He's off to London.'

But Mrs Nancy Pickering did not want anything to do with Tom. She was travelling to see her sister in Surrey and had more important things to think about. 'Right lad, just sit tight and don't get off until you see the signs for 'Kings Cross,' she shouted against the noise, smoke from her Woodbine drifting out of her large nose and crimson mouth at the same time. *I wonder how she does that?* thought Tom, staring at the group of large red spots on her plump left cheek. Tom had tried a dog-end once and had felt so sick that he wondered how people managed with cigarettes. His mam and dad did, in fact all the grown-ups in the village did.

'I've never been to London, Tom,' he remembered his dad telling him. 'They say it's a place where riches are made. You'll be just fine if you remember to stay as you are. Be honest, be careful, and choose friends that you know won't let you down.' He had explained about the Gentleman's Club, Number 100 Piccadilly. 'When you get to the station in London, just wait on the platform, under the clock, for Maisie. She's a maid in the club and will be there to meet you and take you to your new home. I wrote them a letter, and said to look out for a handsome young'un with a straight back and shining shoes, so don't get them dirty mind.'

It all happened in a flash but seemed to take for ever, arms and legs moving slowly, voices distant and muffled, heat and noise. Tom was waving, biting back the burning tears that took over his body. How would he manage so far away from the places he loved? His dad was losing his race to keep up with the steaming train, still waving, tears running down his lined face, dripping onto his thick brown waistcoat. For some reason he had felt that dressing smartly today was the right thing to do, he was so proud of young Tom, but full of worries about his future.

The journey was long. It took over two hours to reach York station, but Tom was mesmerised by the sights through the grey train windows, the trees flying by. At York more people joined his carriage so there were now five, only one seat left. The string luggage slings above the seats were weighed down, but Tom hadn't managed to get his case up there and knew that it took up more than its fair share of room in the carriage. He felt very small and afraid. Loneliness bored painfully into his stomach, but he concentrated hard on stopping his shoulders from hunching and on and holding in the sobs that were about to break through. How was it that everyone else was so sure of themselves? The couple in the corner weren't even talking to each other. Tom wondered about this, his mam and dad didn't talk much either, and when they did the conversation was often angry. Perhaps these two were the same? The pretty woman with flaming red hair might have another fella she cared about more. These thoughts were strangely comforting to young Tom, made him feel that, after all, his world was the same as that of others. Yet he was sure in his heart that he was the only boy on this very long train who was going to London, to a place that he could not even imagine, to do a job that he didn't know how to do, working with people he had never met.

They soon reached Doncaster. Another marker that, further down the line of his life, would play its part in being Tom the husband, and Tom the dad. The sombre-suited grey haired man in the corner pointed and said, with an important air 'Doncaster Cathedral.'

'It's not as good as Durham,' Tom said, unimpressed.

'Well, young man, your voice tells me you are more at home in Durham.'

'How's that?'

'You have a wonderful Geordie accent—but better be careful—in the South they won't know what you're saying,' he chuckled, 'their loss.'

'Mister, I mean Sir, I'm not a Geordie, I'm from Sunderland. What'll I do if that happens and they can't understand me?'

'You look at them with those eyes, hold your head high, walk tall and think a little about their ignorance. You can help them if you think about it and try not to use too many words that will muddle them.'

'Yes, like 'clarts' and 'haway.'

'That's it son, although you may just be surprised at how quickly you'll change. But hang on to who you are, don't get lost in London.'

Tom didn't really know what he meant, but could see that he was trying to be kind. Suddenly, he wasn't alone any more. Like a lost dog, he had found a friend and was not going to let go easily. He could now sleep, with the rhythm of the train drumming in his ears and the haze of smoke filling his lungs that were now stronger. The future would be different.

At Kings Cross, platform four was crowded. There were people pushing their way through, carrying heavy cases, some looking confused, anxiety written all over their faces. His lip trembled; they seemed to be laughing at him, saying things he couldn't understand. This London place was like a foreign country to the frightened young Sacriston boy. Shoulders were hunched, and overcoats pulled tight against the cold September night. Tom looked ahead, down the long platform thronging with people. He clung tightly to his case and hoped that he would be able to spot the big clock. Eddie, one of the footmen, had been sent to collect him instead of the maid he expected. As soon as Tom saw the clock that he had been told to wait under, he hurried to reach it. He stood, a forlorn figure with jet black hair escaping from under the brown shabby cap. A very smart young gentleman was peering in his direction. Could he be looking for him? Surely not, he looked like a rich man, not a servant.

'Are you Thomas?'

'Yes sir, Tom Luccock, that's me,' he stuttered, keen to make a good impression. 'Welcome boy. I'm Eddie glad your train was on time. Now let's get on our way, the car is outside.' A car! Tom had never ridden in a car before. What a day this was. 'Just climb up there,' said Eddie. 'Smart, isn't she? The butler said I should get you back as soon as possible and Betty will sort you out. Of course, you don't know who anyone is, but you'll learn soon enough. We all feel strange at first in a new job.'

'Sir, this is my first real job. I've helped, like on the market, but I only just finished school. Teachers wanted me to stay, mam needed me to get some pay for her.'

'Very tall aren't you Tom? That's why I thought you'd been out in the world. Although, now I can see your face, I can see I made a mistake.'

Tom's case was heavy and it kept hitting his legs. 'Call them legs,' he had often been mocked at school. He'd never liked football, always came home black and blue. But here he was, in the capital of England, the place where the King lived, climbing into a shiny black car with leather seats. They drove slowly, passing shops that were larger than he had ever seen, and buildings that he was sure, must be palaces. Granger Street in Newcastle had some grand places, but nothing like this. 'I remember when I first came down here Tom, I couldn't take it in for a while. But you'll soon get used to it, take it from me. You'll be hopping on and off the tubes as if you were born here.' Tom smiled for the first time that day. So far, everyone had been kind. But he still had to see where he would be working.

100 Piccadilly was a very grand building with even grander members of the Gentleman's Club that it housed. The car drew up in front, just along from the intimidating carved

wooden front doors. 'Down here lad,' said Eddie, taking off his topcoat as he led Tom down some steep steps to a door that was underground. 'This is the way we use. It's mostly open, but if not, try pulling on the bell and someone will let you in.' This door was made of thick oak, but was not as polished and heavy as the main doors. It opened onto a passage with brown lino on the floor. Well, thought Tom, Mam will like this, we've always had brown lino. He was surprised at the lump that jumped into his throat as a picture of home came into his mind.

'Betty, get down here,' shouted Eddie, with a voice that boomed and seemed to shake the walls.

'All right, all right. Where's the fire?' came the laughing reply. Standing in front of him, taking up the whole width of the passageway, was a short, round woman with bright pink cheeks and an even pinker neck. Tom noticed that she had wispy brown hairs on her chin and that her ankles were very fat. 'Hello there, I'm Mrs Nelson, one of the maids from upstairs. Butler has told me to get you sorted out. You can call me Betty if you want, most of the others do.'

Tom's dad had taught him to bow, and this seemed the time to try it out. Betty grinned, took him firmly by the shoulders and pulled him up straight. 'No lad, but that's a promising start. I'll tell you who you need to bow to, but I'm not one of them.'

Tom blushed, and stammered, 'I'm sorry Mrs Nelson,' and then remembered the lines he'd practised with Dad. 'Very pleased to meet you. How are you today?'

Betty broke into laughter, soon accompanied by Jimmy. 'Cor blimey, this one will knock 'em out.' Tom wasn't sure what was going on. He thought it must be all right as everyone was smiling, so he smiled too. Soon he was being led up a winding metal staircase to a long dull room with what looked like a street of beds. Each bed had a rough wooden cabinet at the foot. He soon learned that there were two rooms for the boy servants and two for the maids. Later that night, curled up on his own bed in a room with seven other boys, he tried to fall asleep. Since he was the youngest, his space was the smallest, but everything was vast compared with the terraced house in Sacriston. He wondered how long his bag of sweets - black bullets - that Mam had taken him to buy, would last. Now he was sure she would miss him because she'd bought sweets for him.

'Up at five lad, then you can learn about setting the fires,' said Betty. Tom was good at getting up and was usually the one who pocketed the pence for the first boy up. Tom felt that he already knew all about this work, but soon realised that nothing in Sacriston was this size.

Scuttles had to be filled from the back coalhouse then carried up the wide staircases to all the rooms, even his own. He had slept little, conscious of the other boys around him. His clothes and things he had brought from home were in his own wardrobe at the end of the long room. In here, packed neatly, were the new shirts and trousers that he had been told were his uniform.

'We'll have to get you a proper top coat, this one is too thin and shabby, it'll have to go in the bin,' Betty told him.

He was to have new black shoes and must make them shine, but then, looking down at his present pair, shabby, worn, but mirror-bright even after a long journey from the North, this wouldn't be a problem. 'Well Tom, I can see that you'll be the favourite shoe boy,' said Betty. He was worried that the others in the large house spoke so differently from him. He had a tough time of it with the others in his bedroom. Although he was taller than the rest, they hadn't taken well to his accent, made fun of his attempts to *talk proper*. 'Yer can't talk like this here.' Through the night, in his head, he had tried to say 'make', but it kept coming out 'maek' and the harder he tried the worse it became. Dad didn't tell us about this, he thought.

Days passed quickly. Tom became a Londoner, enjoying the wide pavements of Piccadilly, darting between the crowds on his old roller skates, scuffing his knees like a nine-year-old. Each week he had half a day off. When the weather was bad he paid a penny for the shortest ride on the Underground from Green Park, spending the hours riding around the Circle Line, watching the people, laughing inwardly at some, but more often marvelling at the sadness on the faces. Here in London he had expected everyone to be rich and powerful. Yes, the members of the club he worked in were just what he had anticipated. But ordinary Londoners had the hardest of lives, he thought.

In the club, he was everyone's favourite; always smart, always polite, but with the cheekiest of grins. Sometimes he was told off for whistling. 'Just didn't realise sir, it's when I feel happy, it just happens,' and the under-butler would find it hard to be angry.

Betty began to watch out for him. She would keep him something special back for supper if he'd had a long day, and even bring him treats in from the newspaper shop. 'Our Ernie couldn't eat these, his teeth you know.' This made Tom save his pocket money for a toothbrush. He'd never had one before and Betty showed him how to use soot to make his teeth shine. 'I know it seems daft lad, but you just spit it out, wash out your mouth and look in the glass! They'll be shinier than your shoes, an that's sayin' summat.' His mam and dad had had false teeth, as far as he knew, all their lives. And for Tom too, it was far too late to put right the damage of neglect.

Things went very well. Every Friday he was paid six shillings and three pence. He went to the post office and bought a postal order for five and sixpence and posted it to his mam. After paying for the order and the stamp, he had a little to spend on whatever he wanted. Not everyone was kind to him. He learned to hold his tongue when things were unfair, and sometimes found his own ways to make sure he had the last laugh. There was Nancy, a waitress from the main restaurant. This meant that she was more important than others that worked downstairs. She barked orders, and then complained when they were carried out. She hadn't learned to say thanks. Tom felt that visitors to the club, lords and ladies, and men from Parliament had much to teach her. Some looked down their noses, others ignored the staff, but many engaged in conversation, seeming to be genuinely interested.

Betty had a round and fluffy cat called Percy that lived in the kitchen. This over-fed animal slept a great deal and never caught any mice. 'Percy was my late husband's name,' she said. 'He was fat and lazy, just like this one.'

Tom missed his mam and dad, and even brother George. But George landed on the back step one Sunday in November of that first year. He was waiting there when Tom came in from his tube ride around the city. 'Our George, where did you come from, are you all right? How's Mam and Dad?'

George swaggered, as always, but Tom thought that things weren't good and he felt the stabbing pain in his stomach again. 'Just come to pay yer a visit, but it looks like yer've landed on yer feet. So tomorrow I'll leave.'

'But there's nowhere to stay here. No visitors to staff allowed.'

'Just let us in and ah'll be no bother,' said George, pushing past Tom, who was feeling like a small boy again, lost and powerless. Tom managed to hide George in the big wardrobe. He saved his supper and wrapped it in an old newspaper for his elder brother. George seemed to find this all very amusing, but Tom worried that if he was discovered, he might lose his job and be sent back to Sacriston. This had become a kind of home now. He worked hard but enjoyed the increased responsibilities he was being given. Some of the other boys were jealous, although Tom had such a way about him that any resentment they felt usually evaporated quickly. George left as he had arrived, without any hint of appreciating what Tom had risked, and with no sentiment for his brother or for what the future might hold.

***

In his next job in 1937, a smaller, more elegant residence in Belgrave Square, Tom was already a hit with the ladies of the household. He was there before they asked, seemed to be able to anticipate their needs and then do even more than expected. All of this with his handsome head held proud and high, very different from the bland servitude that they had come to expect. If they were at the theatre, they knew that he would dodge the crowds and have their carriage in the best position to collect them. If it rained, he took special care to make sure that his ladies were kept dry. If it was cold he would bring extra blankets and a flask of tea. Tom didn't seem to realise just how much he appealed to all the women he encountered, he was simply trying to do a good job, to please, to be able to send money to his mam. These days he had more for himself, as tips were large. He also had a wardrobe of fine clothes, including a thick woollen great coat from Saville Row. Promoted to footman, he wore it proudly as he met the ladies after their evenings out, and it was one of the garments that won his Mary over. Back in Sunderland, he would wrap his coat around her as they hurried to escape the shrapnel falling from the skies. Working in The Seaburn Hotel, the skills he learned in London were perfect for the affluent guests.

38

He fell in love with Mary the first time she flounced into the hotel. Night after night he waited for her to come out of the back door of the grand building. At last she agreed to let him take her to the smoky cinema to see a Laurel and Hardy film. That night began a love story that Mary recounted hundreds of times. Tom, three years her junior, was different from anyone else. He was polite and had manners that normal Sunderland boys might have mocked, but to Mary he was perfect. They travelled home on the tram after work every night. Tom would see her to the door and then walk home to the tiny terrace house of his boyhood.

Chapter Three
Meanwhile, in a sleepy corner of Norfolk, 1993

Years rolled by. Our daughters were healthy, leading the lives of country children, playing in meadows, swimming in the nearby lake, building igloos in the snow. But life as a science teacher began to lack excitement for me. Although I knew that I was mostly a good teacher, I had always needed change. One of my weaknesses was not seeing that others sometimes found change difficult. My Master's degree was a chore and did not mean much, but Mary was determined that this would be recognised in the local Sunderland Press. I was horrified but not surprised that she had sent the photo of me at twenty-one in my first robes rather than the new photo of a much older daughter in her new blue robes. That there were more robes ahead, out of the reach of anyone else in the world, would have been a ludicrous thought to Mary or me. Being young and beautiful was always the important thing to Mary. Perhaps she found it hard having two young daughters but she was always proud of them. She had learned how to be a good mother from her own, despite the problems of her childhood. In the same way Tom, the young boy sent to London at fourteen, proved to be a rock of strength and love.

***

'You said you were bored so try this,' said a friend in the staff room of the school where I taught chemistry, as she playfully threw me a sheet of paper. It was about a free trip to Japan to explore culture and education. There would be teachers from countries including Puerto Rico, Russia and Germany. This looked good, but unlikely that I would be chosen. I set about applying and persuading everyone else of the benefits, including my head-teacher. I was astonished to be accepted and set about writing lessons for my time away so that the girls at school would be OK. I was to be one of six Brits; the only science teacher.

My husband Roger drove me to Heathrow and all my childish memories of homesickness returned with a vengeance. The twelve-hour flight left me in Tokyo airport trying to call home, when our younger daughter Rachel croaked to me, 'Mummy I'm feeling sick, please come home.' Yet Rachel recovered and I began the adventure that would change my life and the lives of many thousands of others. I was chosen to represent the British at a meeting with the Japanese Minister for Culture. Waiting outside the Diet (Parliament) I talked to one of the four African people in the group, a charismatic teacher from Ghana, 'from the North,' he stressed. But this meant nothing to me.

He went on to inform me about the problems he faced in school, explaining that he had opened a secondary school for boys and girls, but that it was difficult for girls to get there.

'Why don't we ask the girls from our two schools to write to each other?' I suggested. I was totally ignorant, and unaware that the girls in this African school had been brought up using local tribal languages, and that English, the language of their education, was far from perfect. Nor had I any way of anticipating the changes to lives that would emerge from this chance encounter.

***

Back home in Great Melton, Japan was a million miles away. But the seeds were sewn. 'One of the best parts about the trip was talking to teachers from so many different countries,' I told everyone. And so, at my school, the pupils learned a great deal about Japan. I told them about the day when, standing outside of the Diet (equivalent of our parliament) in Tokyo, the head of a new school in Northern Ghana, Karimu Nachina, asked me how I dealt with things when my pupils died. I was shocked, not knowing how to respond. At that point, my students and I decided that we all might benefit from getting to know, first-hand, about our different societies. Besides, my girls loved the idea of writing to friends living in such a remote place.

***

The first letter arrived, a thin airmail from Ghana. More would follow. Then one day, a simple request: 'do you have any books in your school that you want to throw away? We have none in our school, please can we have them?' I didn't believe this, thinking it a real exaggeration. I began to talk to friends and to the girls I taught, deciding, mistakenly, that collecting old books and sending them out was a simple matter. Another letter told me more. I learned that Wulugu Secondary School had strong buildings, qualified teachers and even, sometimes, electricity. Karimu knew that life for girls was not easy, and that for those who needed to travel and stay near the school, it was hazardous. Many ran away, others, exploited by men from the mud compounds where they boarded, became pregnant – and too many died from clumsy abortions. He wrote;

The majority of girls come from distant villages. They are scattered in local houses at the mercy of illiterate young men. I have on average six pregnancies every three months.

And in another letter;

I am just writing to some organisations for help to build a hostel for the girls with small quarters attached for the mistress who will supervise them. If there is anything you can do about our library it would be appreciated. If your school has any worn-out books, we will accept them with smiles.

And another,

I am sorry to bother you so much with problems of my school but I need to talk them out before I burst with frustration. There are other new schools but most are located in rich communities who know what education is and therefore provide everything. Mine is situated in a very poor community.

Collecting the books was simple at first. In later years when the phone never stopped ringing, when callers would tell me off if I could not drop everything and drive two hundred miles to relieve them of books they wanted rid of, it became a burden. We gathered four tonnes of books, together with a promise to organise and pay for the transport from a local businessman.

The Ghana High Commission were friendly, keen for me to send the books to schools in Accra. But I refused. On the day the books arrived in Wulugu, there was an excited phone call from Francis, the pilot of the small plane that flew them up country on the final leg of the long journey. 'We did it, we did it man!'

'Did what, who are you?'

'I'm Francis, from Race Cargoes. The whole area is in party. There are so many books. No one has ever seen so many books' the rich African voice boomed with excitement.

Francis had been worried about his cargo. This was an unusual trip, and his involvement with transport usually ended at Tamale airport. The short flight from Kotoko to Tamale was always eventful. The runway in the North was rough, and the communication systems rougher. That was bad enough but, like many from the South he was (although he did not like to admit this) afraid of the North. There were stories of ignorance and of tribal wars and barbarism. But if this was true, why should they want books? At the airport he had arranged a truck and a driver to take him to Wulugu. The road that had once existed was now a series of high ridges around deep potholes. They seemed to be travelling to nowhere, but now and then a child appeared, throwing handfuls of sand hopelessly into one of the holes, showing that he was helping fix the road, and then begging for food. There were no other cars, but many people walking barefoot to who knows where? Colourfully dressed women with babies strapped to their backs carried loads on their heads that spread across the road. Children carried broad and deep dishes of water without spilling a drop. Francis thought that this was a waste of time, as the scorching sun must soon evaporate their load. Things were not like this in the city. Far away in rural England I had only a sketchy picture of life in Northern Ghana. I could not begin to know just what an impact we would have on lives, hopes and dreams.

***

'Lynne Symonds Library' said the smart sign over the new school library at Wulugu Secondary School. The roughly made shelves were full of books, sorted into sections.

We have started sorting the books into the various subject areas and are so happy that every subject is covered. Our library will be the richest in Ghana. People or schools don't have a tenth of this and they make a noise about it. We are not making a noise, people who see it make the noise for us. What you call 'old' is brand new to us. Everybody here wants to see you. We don't know how to express our gratitude. Wrote Karimu

Between the shelves were tables and chairs for students to work at. Soon the headmaster realised he needed to keep a careful check. This was the best and largest library in the area and books were going missing. Nine months later when I first entered this building, my feelings of elation soon changed as I realised just how little the school had and how wrong it felt that they wanted and needed our cast-offs.

My African friends warned me not to be arrogant, as education in Northern Ghana was precious. Anything printed on a sheet of paper is better than nothing. I began to see that well-thumbed volumes from schools in England could be treasure troves there.

Over the next few years, countless hours were spent collecting and sorting books. We stocked libraries to many rural schools in Northern Ghana and even helped the impoverished, newly designated, University of Development Studies with its campuses divided across the North. There was constant, friendly help from Rotary Clubs. Officials at the port were demanding, but not receiving, huge sums to release containers. Transport North became more difficult and distribution of books a nightmare, taking the Ghanaian volunteers more time than anyone had anticipated. But fifteen years later, tens of schools were proud of their books. Generous East Anglian volunteers who sorted and packed them knew they had made a real contribution to improving education. At the same time, I looked at 'my' library with shame – so many books had been lost, and others destroyed by dust storms and much use. I was elated when Melinda, a young and enthusiastic science teacher from the American Peace Corps managed to elicit funds to refurbish and re-stock. This was particularly important as Wulugu Sec (as it was affectionately called,) had become a centre for the community, and had many visitors.

Melinda, and before her a succession of VSOs, did their best to improve education at Wulugu Sec. Each year, when we visited, I made a point of finding the VSOs. Often they were in shock at the start of their stay. Despite the very decent accommodation, there was no way of preparing for the weather, the deprivation and the educational need. Even twenty years later, when much had improved, the teachers would know that the child who seemed lazy or tired was simply very hungry, had had no food and had faced a long walk for water before school that day. 'Lynne, our situation is really hopeless here and if I mean to expose every problem to you it will look incredible,' said Karimu. And he was right. 'You see, there is so much difference in the level of civilisation and development between the South and the North. The South has all the wealth and development while the North is still in the Stone Age, trying to catch up. Lynne, you have been so kind to us and we would want you to come and visit. There are National Parks to visit and crocodile ponds. Besides, you can see my school.'

This short request was to bear fruit in years to come. Encouraging help from others I would transform Karimu's school and over a hundred more. We would tackle the endemic poaching that was depleting the largest game reserve in Ghana. Karimu and I would be credited with, in only a short time, making substantial and long-lasting difference to hope and poverty. We would open up education to all girls and women, tackle slavery and increase stability. Our work would change the traditional face of charities. But the road we would travel was perilous, life threatening and terrifying, and seemed to grow longer with every passing year. Karimu's letters often talked of hunger:

This year we are facing severe drought and prospects for farming are bleak, could have been re-written as *every year we have either severe drought or extreme flooding or both.*

None of the mothers had any formal education. Their understanding of basic health and nutrition came from their own mothers and their mothers' mothers. Many of the common practices were harmful. Most children had Kwashiokor, an illness caused by lack of protein, resulting in hugely distended bellies. Lack of calcium made rickets common. Lack of simple hygiene drastically reduced numbers reaching school age. Malaria, Cholera, meningitis and every sort of parasitic infection competed with each other to take young lives where starvation did not.

Karimu told me about the differences between the South of Ghana and the North.

'Southern Ghana had many centuries of contact with the white man. Northern Ghana was only added to the South as a British protectorate in 1900, when the South already had an educated elite. The result of this late contact with the white man is that the North lags behind badly in education and development. In Mamprugu we can count on one hand the university graduates. This, coupled with our lack of natural resources, keeps the North very backward. All things seem to work against the North and Northerners,' Karimu explained. This struck a chord for me. This is what had happened in England. The North was neglected, deprived and severely lacked the educational facilities of the South. It took me back to my own childhood, and thoughts of my mother.

Chapter Four
Mary

A coal-trimmer's work was hot, dangerous and merciless. The dark and dusty coal was guided down the chutes into the holds of the ships in Sunderland port where the trimmer would make sure the load was evenly spread. The River Wear was crowded, the mines were rich, and the merchants traded with speed and greed. Nicholas Scorer was a hard man, never showing fear, never showing pain. His wife May was a dark-haired beauty who had been wooed by his strong presence and then fell into marriage already carrying their first boy. There were more boys, then three girls, with Mary the last but one. The youngest girl, Vickie, developed a defect that meant she would always have the mind of a child. May was a wonderful cook, learning from her German mother. She could make a feast from faggots, and even then was always the one who would help the beggars in the street. There were too many children for their tiny home in Dunning Street right beside the River Wear, yet she sometimes allowed a tramp or two to stay in the cellar, saying, 'God wants us to care for each other.'

Mary was a pretty child. In Commercial Road school she couldn't make much sense of arithmetic, but came into her own writing stories. Mary was hoping for a fairy tale life and snatched glimpses of dreams, using her mind to escape from some of the battles and beatings in the back yard at home. So, when cousins from the music halls visited, it was Mary who preened and danced for them, and Mary who wanted to be one of them. Of course, May would never let her go with these people, with their make-up and fancy clothes. She loved her girls so much, perhaps even more now that her husband had become so angry with life. Mary was always spotless, and carried a clean white handkerchief every day for hygiene inspection. She didn't like anything that was unpleasant, from spiders to bad language, and somehow never learned to face the reality of illness or unhappiness. At thirteen she left school to work in Mrs Doyle's fruit and vegetable shop. Her mam found her the job after promising that she would attract customers since she was so pretty. The boys had gone off to do their time in the army and had learned good trades. Eddie and Ralph were electricians and found work in Maidstone. Harry stayed near to his parents. No one spoke about Vickie, now living in an austere 'mental asylum' near Morpeth. May did not have the bus or train fare to visit.

The boys in Maidstone were increasingly worried about their sisters, and their, sometimes difficult, home life. They decided to take this into their own hands and wrote to May, enclosing train fares for the girls to come down South. May was grateful but distraught. These days were black days, her still young body was thin, and she limped from an injury that would not heal. Deep inside, she felt that this was right for her girls, but that they might never come home. What she did not know, was that they would come home to bury her.

Mary still dreamed. In the Dog and Gun in Maidstone she worked hard and got on well with the family, particularly Mr Sneddon, her boss. She enjoyed polishing the glasses until they sparkled, and her work in Doyle's had shown her that she could add up in her head. In many ways, this work was easier as she did not need to calculate the weight of half or a quarter of a pound. Mary lived in with the family, and had her own room for the first time in her life. Although the winter was cold, she managed without a warm coat so that she had more to spend on dresses. She scoured the market for bright colours and shapes that would show off her figure; tight at the waist, not too high at the front. She earned the nickname *The Boxley Road Mannequin* and was flattered by this. She would take the train to visit Marjorie who, being the eldest, had been found a job that paid more, in The Stoneleigh, an up-market hotel in Surbiton. She and Marjorie would often swap clothes and shoes. They were the best of friends and their times together were spent laughing and exchanging stories about the people they served drinks to. Mary was vulnerable and gullible. May prayed so hard each night that she would be safe. She had warned both of her girls of the dangers they would face and made them promise never to drink alcohol. Mary was beautiful, but, deep-down, she needed constant confirmation of this.

The girls worked together for a time. Mary had to leave The Dog and Gun when Mrs Sneddon's jealousy began to make her husband ill natured, so Marjorie persuaded her boss to take Mary on. The two girls together behind the bar brought increasing trade and there were large tips so that more money could be sent home to May. Mary was continually flattered by the attention of the customers, and although most were much older than her dad, she played to the audience.

May's letters were short these days. Mary began to worry that Dad was not looking after her. And then it came, the letter from Harry telling the girls that Mam was very ill and that they needed to come home. But the girls arrived too late to say their goodbyes. May was far too young to die and they were far too young to be left without their Mam. Marjorie went back South but Mary looked for work at home. Someone needed to be there now to do the woman's work and Mary, being the youngest, was expected to do this. If only she had learned more from her own Mam. She knew how to make pies, ham and egg and mince and potatoes, but had no idea about cooking roast meat or even vegetables. She was glad when Dad brought in a woman to clean and cook, and even more pleased when the chance to work behind the bar in the very best hotel in Sunderland presented itself.

'Fancy Mam,' she whispered in bed that night. She talked to her mam every day, shared all her secrets, and knew that she was looking after her from heaven. Mam was sure about heaven and had told Mary what a beautiful place it would be, where everyone was kind and no one cold or hungry. 'I went in there,' she told her, 'round the back door like they told me, and all these fellas were looking at me. I just smiled at them all and asked a waiter where the manager was and told him I was after a job. Then he took me through a big wooden door to Mr Finkle's office - he's the boss - and told me to sit and wait. I felt dead scared Mam, so I held tight onto the chair and that helped a bit. Mr Finkle isn't from here, I mean not from England, he speaks funny and I couldn't get what he was on about at first. Then he slowed down and I knew that he was telling me about the hours I'd need to be at work. The tram goes from the end, you know, near the last steps down to the sea, so that'll be fine, even if I finish at half ten sometimes. Then he took me to the bar. Honest Mam, it's a really posh place, I don't think you'd have been in there. The thing is, the girls behind the bar are a bit pushy. They have to wear navy overalls, but it looks to me that some of them have nothing on underneath. I sort of said that I might not fit, but Mr Finkle said he really wanted me to start tomorrow and the pay is better than the Stoneleigh. Then Mary pulled off her thin navy skirt and blue cardigan and quickly dressed for bed, shivering with worry. She told herself that tomorrow would be the start of the rest of her life.

The tram was packed that Monday afternoon, a lovely summer's day, with mothers and children carrying buckets and spades and picnics down to the sea front. Mary was early, so she knelt on one of the concrete benches overlooking the sea, over the road from the imposing Seaburn Hotel. The air rang with shouts and laughter as small boys and girls ran into the sea, but quickly ran back as the biting cold waters covered their feet. Somehow the warmth of the sand made the water feel even colder. The sand was thick with square green tents, weighted down by sand in the pockets round their bases. Mary could not think why there were so many tents, they were often a shelter from the harsh weather but today was beautiful. She watched as a steady queue of mothers, dressed in bright cotton dresses, formed by the hot water kiosk. They paid a penny to have boiling water poured into the large metal teapots they had carried from home. Often the tea dregs were used over again, so that by the end of the day what came out of these pots was little more than stained water. This, along with meat paste sandwiches, was the standard fare of the day. The sandwiches were warm, flattened, and had a sprinkling of yellow sand. But they tasted good, and few could pay the two pence for chips, or buy a penny cornet from Notarianni's ice cream parlour. It was the youngsters that did these things, the young people who had jobs and no families to feed.

Further along the sea front, on the same side of the road as the hotel, was the new fairground. Mary could just hear the music, although the waves were noisy as they pushed the stones up the beach. Mary loved to walk around the fairground, fascinated by the slot machines, the waltzer and the whine of the ghost train. She and her brother Eddie had once had a ride on the shuggy boats but the swinging motion had made her feel sick. Eddie had been impatient with her, but stopped to let her out and carried on alone until the elderly man in charge called time. Now Mary decided it was time to go, time to cross the road, walk to the side entrance and try to find Mr Finkle. As she crossed the wide hallway, a tall, very dark young waiter darted in front of her. Mr Finkle appeared at the same time, welcoming her in his broken English. 'Miss Scorer, we are glad you are here,' he said, as the waiter, returning with a loaded tray, approached. 'Oh Thomas, this is Miss Scorer, our new girl in the bar.'

Mary smiled at him, a smile suggesting, look at me, I'm beautiful. 'Yes, I'm Mary Scorer.' And that was it for Thomas. Despite his good looks and the self-assurance he'd developed in London, he had never really paid too much attention to women. He did not want to become involved. After all, he could see how unhappy this had made others. But this girl fascinated him. She was all he could think about. As days went on, he would do anything just to see her. He changed his shifts to fit in with Mary's and began to catch the same tram, so it was easy to talk to her at the stop. If it rained, he would wait for her and shelter her under his black umbrella. Better still, if it was cold, he would wrap her round with his Saville Row great coat, and Mary felt warm and secure. Mary was flattered by his manner, so different from the other boys around the North, more like the 'toffs' that visited the Stoneleigh, yet not like them at all. Tom treated her just as she imagined a real lady would like to be treated. Even at The Seaburn, he did everything he could to make things easier for her, stepping in to carry a heavy tray, being at her side when there were so many glasses to wash. Mr Finkle noticed this and smiled quietly. His customers were fond of Thomas, often asking for him by name, and probably tipping him well for seeing quickly to their requests for cabs or pressed clothes. These days, 'The Seaburn' was the pride of Sunderland. All the Empire Theatre stars stayed here, and the hotel's reputation was growing. Tom valued the time Mr Lowrie spent talking to him as he had been told that this man was a famous painter.

Mary might have been easy prey for some of the men who frequented the bar, but Mary was safe with Tom.

If tips were good, Tom and Mary would go to the Regal cinema to watch anything that was playing. In the old and smoky cinema, they only had eyes for each other. The smoke was coloured blue by the wall lights that guided the customers. Programmes ran without intervals or breaks, so getting to seats needed an usherette with a torch. The same usherette would walk up and down the aisles with her tray of choc-ices and tubs. Money and orders were passed along rows and the ices passed back again. If you were at the wrong end, the ice cream that reached you could have its chocolate coating broken into pieces, with some of the vanilla ice dripping out of the foil wrapper. It was at the cinema that Tom and Mary caught up with the news. As war threatened in 1938, watching Pathe News clips about soldiers preparing to leave England made it very real indeed; then the closing of the beaches, blocking entrances to this peaceful part of the shoreline. Mary was very good at blotting out the parts of life that she did not want to face, and so she and Tom, like many others, would stay outside during the air raids that became increasingly frequent. Foolishly at times they would sit on a bench in Mowbray

Park watching the skies light up. Sometimes they would run and dodge shrapnel.

Inevitably the day came when Tom received his call-up papers. It was the air force that he wanted to join and he was sure that he'd be a pilot. Mary didn't believe it would actually happen. 'When you go to war, I'll write to you every day,' she said. 'Will you send me presents from the places you go?' Tom could not imagine that there would be shops. He knew that his pay would mostly be sent and spent by his mam and Uncle Bob. They were living in a pitman's cottage near Doncaster now, leaving Tom's dad in Sunderland. Bob had been coughing more lately, something that all pitmen did.

Tom came back from his medical feeling rejected and incomplete. The brave young man who was to fly in combat for his country, had failed the eyesight test. 'Almost, but not quite A1 bonny-lad, so it's ground support for you. Training at Blackpool, then wait and see.'

Mary thrilled at his uniform, proud to stand beside him as he waited for the truck to carry him to Blackpool. She had left the hotel job now and joined the workers on the benches at the munitions factory at Birtley. The girls were rough and robust, wearing bright overalls and turbans over their tightly permed hair. They were all shapes and sizes, and Mary was glad that they were so friendly. She was unaware that some of the girls imitated her way of walking, and that proud tilt of her head. Girls on the bomb case line all stuck together and there were many strong friendships starting up, several that would far outlive marriages as husbands lost their lives, dying in pain and terror so far away from their families. Somehow, the deaths and hardships drew the factory girls together. They sat at the long benches, laughing and swapping stories. At first, Mary simply couldn't hear anything. The noise from the neighbouring galvaniser's yard seemed overwhelming. But as time went on, she learned to hear both the talk and the songs. One song would begin at the bottom end of the huge expanse of building, increasing in loudness and feeling, until the whole air was filled with the voices of five hundred women:

It's a long way to Tipperary, *Run Rabbit Run* or *We'll meet again*. Somehow this was better than the singing in the shelters, even without the men. The girls' work was vital to the war effort. Bomb cases had to be filled carefully to avoid an explosion that would destroy them all. But they still managed to break rules, often enclosing messages to the airmen, tucked inside the bomb case with the live charge. Mary, who had been promoted to the post of 'Inspector of Armaments' by a boss with an eye for pretty girls, had enjoyed the work inspecting bomb cases, almost as much as she enjoyed the camaraderie and singing. The girls became oblivious to the constant noise from the galvaniser's yard next door, but this was a major problem for many later in life when their hearing began to fail.

Tom's father George, worried about Mary. He could see that it would be challenging for her to resist advances while Tom was away. He often made excuses to call by, to meet her from work, but Mary avoided him whenever she could.

He was kind and gentle and soon realised that Mary was, along with her friends, enjoying the harmless attentions of the American troops who swaggered around the streets, whistling at the girls and offering chewing gum and cigarettes. Everyone smoked. Mary knew that wives were sending parcels to their husbands through the forces postal service. She planned a small parcel with things that would be useful, deciding to send Tom some Woodbines as a treat. But she couldn't spend much. Things like lipstick and stockings were expensive and essential.

When the war ended, the factory closed. Mary found temporary work in shops as she expected her Tom to be home soon, taking care of everything. It was a long, long year between the end of the war and troops from Burma being sent home in 1946.

Chapter 5
War and Marriage

Tom ached with despair. His Mary was so beautiful, yet he had to leave her. He knew that she'd not begun to think about what their separation would mean. He also knew that, once he was gone, Mary would have many temptations. She was a natural flirt, nothing serious, but Tom was jealous. This is why he had proposed to her so soon, desperate to make sure that they would stay together. He had borrowed the money from his mam, and he knew she would want it back soon, and with interest. Mary was three years older than Tom and a survivor, very much like Tom's mam, but neither of them saw this. Mary had always wanted a platinum ring. 'But don't worry if you can't afford that Tommy pet'. He lay awake at night, certain that he could never meet her expectations, but he worshipped her. The ring was tiny, with a square setting that had a diamond that was the smallest in the shop. But it was platinum, and if Tom traded his watch and lived on five shillings for a month, he could do it.

It was all worth it when Mary's eyes sparkled with pleasure. She knew how much Tom loved her already, but felt that this was proof. None of the boys and men she had met before treated her as a precious flower, to be cared for and cherished the way Tom did. How proud he would have been had he known that their three grand-daughters would each wear that ring as they were married.

***

'The name's Peter Lord, but pals call me Lordie,' said the stocky cadet sitting next to him, in a strong and cheerful voice. 'We're on our way now. You ever been to Blackpool before? Best chip suppers they say.'

'I'm Thomas, and no, never been to Blackpool. Wonder where we'll be staying?' Lordie and Tom were to spend much of the war together. First in the attic of a seaside bed and breakfast, lying side by side across the bare boards with eight others. Later, they would look back on these days as luxurious. Training was challenging. His boots fitted badly and the uniform scratched Tom's skin. He realised that his London work clothes had been of high quality; dulling his memory of the rags he grew up in.

***

'Bombed out' were the only two words on the telegram that the sergeant brought Tom.

'Nothing too serious I hope, son?' he asked.

'Sir, my fiancé's home has been bombed, they've lost everything. I must go.'

Four days of leave followed. Mary had ignored the air-raid warnings, hiding under the wooden kitchen table with Joey the budgerigar. The roof was blown off. Curtains were found a mile away along the railway track. Everything was destroyed, but Mary, dusty and shocked, was hardly hurt. The factory girls helped Mary and her family, and shared what they could with them. Although the house collapsed and all the contents were damaged, Mary was lucky to be alive.

The family were given two rooms at Grangetown. The bits of furniture that neighbours further along Sandringham Terrace helped them pull out of the rubble were enough, as the new place was very small. But all of her precious memories of Mam were gone. The few photographs and letters lost, and Mam's favourite blue dress, the one with the cap sleeves and lace on the belt was in shreds. But for Mary, having her handsome boyfriend home almost made it worth it. 'Come on Tommy, tell me all about the Air Force.'

Tommy felt that he didn't know much yet. He had learned to march, to load and clean a rifle and to run carrying a heavy pack. He'd also learned that those in charge were different from him; spoke with posh accents but did not behave like gentlemen. In London, Tom had watched and listened and felt that true gentlemen were polite to everyone, even the kitchen boys. They talked about their wedding. Mary had dreamed, as all girls did then, of a white dress in the chapel. She would make her dad so proud, and Vickie would be allowed to come. Dear Vickie, she missed her so much but had ben assured that she was happy in the special hospital for those who were not quite the same as others.

It was to be a rushed wedding with a special license. What about my dress? What about the cake? She wept for her mam. 'Mam, I can't tell him I feel like this. I love him so much, but to get married now, before he goes to war, it's too rushed.'

***

Wearing a smart grey suit, very high heels and a hat decorated with bluebirds, Mary walked down the aisle of Christ Church. She had made a real effort to draw straight stocking seams with eyebrow pencil up the back of her legs. Friends and neighbours had worked hard, had given them ration coupons and dried fruit, so there was even a wedding cake. Tom glowed with pleasure at the sight of Mary. He felt what a lucky man he was, and tried to forget that he only had four days with his bride. But those days laid down memories that would last forever. They took the train to Leicestershire, to Auntie Muriel's tiny cottage. She was a kindly, smiling lady whose cottage was surrounded by July flowers. 'My dears,' she said, 'this is your home; I'll not be bothering you. There's food in the pantry, I've bought some special boiled ham. Just have what you want and I'll be back on Wednesday.' And so Tom and Mary spent three days and nights together before the war separated them.

***

Tom was sent to York to finish his training, and then on to Liverpool to sail. The people thronging on the dockside were mostly servicemen, traders, sweethearts and mothers. Tom was alone, feeling frightened and afraid, just as he'd felt as a boy in London; yet this was much worse.

Then, out of the crowd, came a voice he recognised. 'You lost Tom? Think we both are, maybe we can find bunks close to each other.'

'Lordie, where have you been? How come we're on the same ship?'

'Luck of the draw lad, haway, let's get on.'

Tom and Lordie found hammocks in the engine room, which was hot, noisy and crowded. It would be home for the two-week voyage. Tom discovered he was a good traveller with a sturdy stomach, something that was to change a few years later. But for now he ate heartily while others were crippled with seasickness. He made a friend of the ship's cat, a creature that found him a constant source of snacks, learning to find Tom whenever he whistled. Tom had never had a pet cat and decided that, once this war was over, he would find a ginger kitten for Mary and himself. They would have babies, but still have room for their pet cat. The seas were rough and the days were dull, with little to do but talk and think, and think and talk. Some of the men seemed brash and brave, but most were scared. All were unsure of their destination but there were rumours of India and Burma, places that meant nothing to men who had never left their own hometowns or villages before call-up, let alone England. The Suez Canal was something they never thought they'd see.

The boat docked in India. The men were loaded into trucks, still uncertain of where they were heading, and trundled slowly towards the base camp in Burma. The base was like nothing Tom had ever seen before. Hot, damp air, lush green trees, and thick grass. There were mountains behind and snakes in the grass. Tat RAF Hmawbi, Yangoon, Tom was shown his hut, along with the prisoners of war who would take care of him. Surely, this couldn't be right, these men seemed gentle and smiling, not at all the picture he had in his head of the 'vicious Japs.'

'Don't trust them, though, or they'll knife you,' his sergeant warned, then showed Tom where he'd be working on aircraft maintenance. Tom's hopes of flying were less important to him now. Newsreels reported that flyers were being shot down in large numbers.

He wrote to Mary every day, and was allowed to send the letters each week. It helped him to feel that he was talking to her, but had to be careful not to reveal what was happening at the camp. Mary wrote to Tom too. But each time the post came there was nothing for him. After four months, all Mary's letters arrived in one delivery. Tom was ecstatic. Mary also sent him a parcel with smokes, some shoe polish, soap, and a handkerchief.

For four long years they fought their war apart, Mary in munitions, Tom in Asia. Tom became thin and tanned. He was kind to everyone, whistling through days and sleeping well at night. He was fit, worked hard and was well liked by all, even the Japanese prisoners of war at the air base. Tom realised that these men were in a strange land far from those they loved, just like him. He found it hard to think that they were of the same nationality that was treating his own countrymen so cruelly. Tom also liked the locals who worked at the camp, particularly the Chai Wallahs. In the years that followed he would often call out 'Chai Wallah' when making hot drinks for Mary and his family. When the war ended, they all thought they'd be on their way home.

But there was still work to be done in Burma, so there was another very long year until he was taken to the ship that would carry him home.

***

He was nervous when he saw Mary waiting at Sunderland Railway station. It was four years since their wedding day, and the briefest of honeymoons. Mary was nervous too. She dressed carefully that morning, as she always did, but when their hands met on the cold station platform, she knew it would all turn out well. They walked hand in hand to the bus that took them to her father's house, now near Roker Park football ground. It had a sitting room, kitchen and two small bedrooms.

***

Tom looked for work and was pleased to be accepted by Sunderland Borough Police Force. His air force reference was excellent, and his experience with Japanese prisoners was valuable. After training he became Constable 91, and Mary became pregnant. 'You need to find somewhere else to live before the baby comes,' said the midwife. There's T.B. in the house, you can't have a baby here. Mary's dad – my granddad - was very unwell with tuberculosis. There was no cure. His life as a coal trimmer had made him susceptible to illness. I have a hazy memory of him when I was very small, so he must have visited at least once before he died.

Chapter Six
Chester Road

The upstairs rented flat in 164 Chester Road, was our first home. Tom's police pay was low, but at least he had a job. The rent allowance covered the costs of the simple flat with its kitchen and bedroom. The kitchen was also the living room, a large room with a bay window overlooking the road. Tramcars ran outside the front door and made it easy for the family to get into town. Tom had found them a solid, square, oak table and two chairs. They had a comfortable settee from the second-hand shop nearby, a tin box oven in the corner, and some odd plates and cups. On the landing there was a large cupboard. This is where they kept their buckets of water and coal for the fire. In winter they lit the fire in the kitchen, and, if anyone was unwell, the tiny grey hearth in the bedroom glowed with cheer. The tap in the back yard next to the outside toilet was shared with the family that lived downstairs. Tom and Mary had their own coalhouse, with a small opening onto the back lane for delivery. The cobbled back lane was a playground for the children to come. But now there were only older children, as there had been no chance to make babies with the men away at war. Tom and Mary loved their flat, searching for pictures for the wall in St Gabriel's Church jumble sales. Tom made clippie mats for the floor and Mary knitted cardigans, hats and bootees for me. Mary would unravel old woollens bought from jumble sales, wash the wool, and make it into new clothes. Food was still rationed but Tom made sure that Mary had her share.

In August 1947, I was born in the General Hospital in Chester Road, just beside St Gabriel's. Our small family were unaware that their lives would always return to Chester Road, and here they would die, and rest in their coffins. Chester Road had everything they needed. 'Oh what a beautiful morning, oh what a beautiful day' sang Maisie, a generously built, rosy-cheeked Sunderland girl, busily scrubbing the floor in the corridor outside the maternity ward as Tom rushed in to see me, his new daughter. He would remind me of this moment many times. Mary worked harder than she had ever done in her life. Pails of water heated in pans on the fire to wash the nappies had to be carried up the steep stairs, and washed in the sink, but at least they had a drain to the outside. Tom had done extra shifts at the football matches through the winter to help them to buy the things they needed. Mary's sister's boy was now six, so she'd handed over bundles of bedding and clothes, as well as a cot, much better than the drawer they'd first put me in.

I was a placid baby. Mary soon regained her figure and enjoyed the extra attention a baby brought as she played with me in Burn Park. Sometimes she would make up my bottle and a picnic and stay for hours. She had learned not to mind that Tom was working shifts, but found herself recalling boys she had met before Tom. Tom was the love of her life, but daydreams were far more glamorous than the harsh realities of the upstairs flat. The day she met

Freddie Wheeler again, by chance, fuelled her memories but there were no regrets. They'd had a date before the war, and were due to meet at the Regal Picture House. Mary had spent hours getting ready, wearing her new black high heels and borrowing perfume from her sister. But Freddie had stood her up.

'It's Mary, isn't it?' he asked, 'and with a baby.'

'Yes Freddie, and you stood me up.'

'No, I waited, but you never came.'

They found out that they'd waited at different cinemas that night.

'I wonder what would have happened to us if we'd met?' said Freddie. 'You know how much I cared for you,' he said, looking straight into her green eyes. 'My wife's waiting for me.' And then he was gone. As I became a toddler, our tiny flat was the centre of my world. Daddy played wonderfully imaginative games with me, making forts under the kitchen table, and tents with blankets draped over chairs. I loved the toy cars he bought me, and we would make roads from cardboard and building blocks. Sometimes Mary found it hard entertaining me when Tom was at work. She thought carefully, and decided that she needed to talk Tom into finding the money for nursery school. Miss Ritchie's nursery school at the top of Chester Road was quite cheap. I would make friends and learn to read.

'You see Tom,' said Mary, 'she only has the yard to play in and I don't like leaving her there on her own. That woman downstairs is very strange, and her daughter has illegitimate twins.' Tom agreed. The pattern of giving in to Mary was well established. In later years, thinking back over his life, he often wondered when he began to give Mary her own way in everything, deciding that this had not really been the best plan, and suspected that many husbands did that to ensure a peaceful life.

***

I never really understood what 'Miss Ritchie's' nursery school was all about. We had to sit at desks and keep quiet, and I just waited for Mam to come back. After a girl bit my arm one day and my teacher told me to bite her back, Mary changed her mind about Nursery school and I spent the days when Tom was at work shopping with Mam or happily playing in the yard. The favourite shop, over the road from 164, and half way to the hospital, was the *Co-op*. Here they served butter from a huge block and poured sugar into blue paper bags. Nearby was the *People's Dispensary for Sick Animals.* They sometimes had pets for sale in the window and I was fascinated by the rabbits and kittens. Mam bought wool from Kemps—the only one of those early shops still open half a century later.

Nearer to the house, just up the road, was *Andersons,* a sweet shop, selling everything a child could dream of. There were rows of sweets in jars and piles of chocolate. Next door to this, the Chinese laundry starched Dad's blue police shirt collars. I had seen pictures of the Chinese professor in my *Rupert Bear* books, so a visit to the laundry was very exciting. Mam was friendly with all the shopkeepers, and seemed to spend hours talking to Mrs

Doyle in the tiny greengrocery, where brightly coloured fly-papers hung from the ceiling coated with the remains of long dead flies. Sometimes there was not much on sale, for Mrs Doyle had a grown-up son to keep, and it was hard to have the money she needed for food. Once she brought a fur coat to show Mary. 'You would look lovely in this pet. Try it on, I'll sell it to you cheap.' But even Mary, who wanted so many things, knew she did not live in a fur coat world. Over the road, next to Chester Road School, was *Shellings* the pork butchers. Meat was a luxury, but the sausages were fat and salty. I loved to kick the bloodied sawdust around the floor, and seeing the strings of sausages hanging on hooks from the ceiling.

The family downstairs were noisy. They threw rubbish up the stairs and used language that Tom and Mary did not want me to hear. I never heard my parents swear. They were delighted when their kindly landlord, Mr Waugh, told them that the downstairs flat next door, number 162, would soon be empty. This had more room, with, to Mary's delight, a proper front room. She was also determined to have a real carpet. So Tom cut down on cigarettes and got behind with the rent to buy a roll of rich red carpet. This was kept rolled up, but laid down when the room was used. Which was hardly at all apart from my birthday parties.

Behind the kitchen was a scullery with a proper gas cooker. A bath ran along one wall with a wooden cover that was taken off each week when I was bathed. There was an electric boiler to heat the water, but the process was very slow. Mary preferred to strip off in front of the kitchen fire with a bowl of water, but Tom did not often wash. The outside toilet in the yard froze over in the winter. Tom built a shed in the back yard from old orange boxes. He wasn't much of a handyman but my friends and I spent many hours in that shed.

***

Above us lived the Sheridans. Mrs Sheridan worked for *Milburns* the bakers and often brought home bread and cakes. Mr Sheridan was totally blind and bed bound, so Mary would take him a cup of tea and sit and chat. She was very kind. One of my earliest memories was of stroking the cat on the window-ledge beside old Mr Sheridan's bed. One day Dad brought a ginger tabby home from the *PDSA* and called him Sandy. Sandy spent much of his time sitting on my lap.

Peter Allun and Edward Metcalf lived next door, at 160 Chester Road. The Metcalfs were all small and wiry and Edward's dad had trouble with his chest. The Alluns were stocky and fair, and weren't in debt, unlike so many others in the row of terrace houses. Peter's dad was a dental technician, his mam kindly. Peter lived there with his mam long after his dad died, caring for her night and day. This unlikely trio of children spent their days together. Games of cowboys and Indians seemed to last forever. Watching the flies buzz around the gaslights in Peter's house was hypnotic, as I began to realise that there were other people who were important to Mam and Dad. In the back yard I learned to skip, with Mam tying one end of the rope to the drainpipe. 'Polly in the kitchen, doing a bit of stitching, in came the bogy man and chased Polly out,' we'd chant. The back lane behind the yard and the coal shed was a constant source of adventure. We played on the cobblestones, dodging the coal carts with their black bags of fuel unloaded by strong men ingrained with coal dust. We were content, unaware of the poverty and hardship of our parents, feeling safe and loved. The world was ours. No one had heard of holidays, and the highlight of the weekend was the reading of the football scores on the wireless, hoping we'd predicted the necessary eight draws. Tom carried on with *Vernon's Pools* for many years, and the family always hoped.

At five years old I was taken on a trip to Kent with Mam and her sister. It was a long, slow journey that took a whole day. In Maidstone we were greeted with smiles and love from childless Elsie, wife of Mary's brother Ralph. I met other distant relatives, including Eddie, the second brother to move to Kent. Eddie was married to Doris and they had a son Nicholas who stayed in touch for most of his life.

***

Chester Road School was an ageing but impressive building, looming across the road from 162. It simply never occurred to me that this was anything to do with me, until September 1952 when I found myself standing in a large room full of strange children all gripping onto a mother's hand, many crying loudly. 'Lynne Luccock,' someone called across the room, and Mam pushed me towards the small stout teacher who had called out my name. I tried hard not to cry. I did not understand what was happening.

I had a clean handkerchief and Mam had given me some toilet paper and aspirins 'just in case'. I had no idea what this meant, only knowing that they were not in a case, and that perhaps I should have one. Margaret 'Peggy' Ellis was a kind but firm teacher in the infants' school. The children were sat in their places around low tables but allowed to move onto the carpet for story time. I quickly learned to read, and could already write my name. Some of my friends boasted about how clever they were but no one could do sums as well as me. Peggy never had children of her own. Over fifty years later she was to read about me in the local *Echo,* and when she died, left a small legacy for me to help build a school in northern
Ghana.

My dad, Tom and I played with numbers for hours. It was one of my favourite games and I was surprised that other people in my class did not seem to enjoy adding and multiplying. But I was very jealous of those who could draw pictures, and even more of those who were not afraid to answer questions out loud. In those days of scabby knees and measles, it was what happened in the toilets that posed one of the greatest health hazards. The long row of outside cubicles had a corridor and wooden doors that did not reach the ground. Groups of girls - perhaps the ballerinas of the future - would spend hours creating tableaux by standing on the toilet seat, the cistern or the door ledge. Hands touched every part of the toilet and if there were wash-basins they were never used. In winter the cold air anaesthetised the smell of the often-blocked toilets. In summer, nothing could disguise the stench, but the girls still played and laughed, oblivious of the smell that stayed on their clothes and shoes throughout the day.

I skipped home each dinnertime. The best days were when Dad was on 'point duty', manning the zebra crossing to make sure the children could cross safely between the trams and occasional car. I supposed it was called 'point duty' as he had to point at cars and tell them when to move or stop. He was tall, proud and handsome and I held onto his white-gloved hand tightly as he guided the group of children the short distance to safety. Other children were in awe of me having a copper for a dad. Often, when he was on a two to ten shift, Mam watched him leave home to walk miles to a 'beat' (the area he was working in) where shelter was rare and his heavy cloak would soon become heavier, soaked with relentless Sunderland winter rain. I loved to go to the police station on Friday with him, standing in line with the men waiting to collect their weekly pay. This was always a happy day. Together we would walk down High Street into Fawcett Street, spend a few pence in Woolworths on a new toy, then rush for the tram to get home to play. I felt the luckiest of girls, having a dad that was such a special man but found it difficult to deal with his health problems. Once, when he had lain moaning at night and was carried off to hospital, I experienced a devastation that was to return often but I never learned to deal with it. Mam was told to boil all the bedclothes to prevent infection. This simply could not be done in the flat. She did her best but wanted him back to show that he was well again. Luckily, his time for full recovery from this meningitis scare was short.

***

Mary managed the household budget carefully. There was even money for Sarsaparilla and cream soda. Rationing meant that sweets bought from *Andersons* were rare, but there were broken biscuits from *Woolworths,* and Tom often had the local 'Creamola' toffee factory on his beat and would bring home a bag full of mis-shapes. Mary and Tom lost their teeth before they were 35. It was cheaper to have them taken out than treated. Neither had owned a toothbrush and they often allowed me to skip my teeth cleaning. All my friends had had teeth removed. The experience was cruel and terrifying, involving a gas mask, but somehow OK as everyone went through it. I felt so sick afterwards. Mam struggled to deal with unpleasant things but knew she could rely on Dad to made sure I had a present as I left the dentist, so that I would be willing to return if necessary.

***

School work was not difficult at this stage. I wrote long stories and loved doing sums, but was timid, afraid to speak up and afraid of anything that attracted attention to me. I was taller than others, even the boys, despite being the youngest in the class. People expected me to be more grown-up, and I obliged as best I could. School brought new friends and birthday parties. 162 was a magical place for birthdays. The roll of carpet was put down in the front room, and a large table borrowed with a dozen chairs. The table was laid with sandwiches, twiglets, cakes and scones. Milburn's delivered the cakes, but Mary made the scones. They were hard, and the currants on the outside burned. Inside was the treat, a coin wrapped in greaseproof paper. Everyone brought presents and everyone left with one. The girls wore the prettiest of dresses and the boys had polished shoes. The best part of the party was the games, where Tom's love for children came into its own, steering them through pass the parcel, musical chairs, statues and forfeits amid the non-stop laughter of an age of innocence. Tom played 'Paddy Says' with such delight, the children laughing so much that it didn't really matter who got it right or who lost—they just wanted more. They clapped, shouted, shrieked and simply were. In an age of hardship, this, for me, was the party of all parties. The year that Nana, (Elizabeth, dad's mother), brought my party dress was the best of all. It was white taffeta with tiny pink rosebuds. I had never seen anything so beautiful.

When Sandy the cat went missing, I looked everywhere, distraught, and asked everyone. Much later I learned that he had an incurable skin disease. Tom's mother visited more often, bringing Uncle Bob with her. I loved to go to stay at their colliery house near Doncaster. The backs of the houses surrounded a communal green where children and dogs played. The women shared common hardships and the men spent their off-duty time in the club, quenching their miners' thirst with cold beers. I enjoyed the trips to Woodlands, watching Nana cook on the hearth and smelling the coal dust that seeped everywhere.

Everyone smoked Players or Woodbines, unaware of any danger, there had been no research then, and certain that, in the hardest of times, this was a necessity of life.

Nana and Bob went on holiday with us all. When I was seven we took the train to Bridlington, and a year later to Scarborough. The bed and breakfasts were a long walk from the beach, but the beaches and boats were fascinating. I learned to play Bingo, and that Mam liked Frankie Vaughan.

***

Chester Road Junior school treated the children firmly and kindly as it began their preparation for life. We sat in single rows, forbidden to talk to each other. We all did the same work at the same time.

Brenda Pearson taught fifty girls in a windowless attic room, separated by a sliding partition from fifty boys.

How she managed to encourage large numbers of us to succeed in the eleven plus exam is unfathomable. Brenda and I reconnected over sixty years later, thanks to a mutual friend from Sunderland Rotary Club. Many of her students became medics or academics but for children like us, at this time, it would have seemed impossible. Things were changing rapidly in post-war Sunderland. I was given a lot of freedom, travelling into town alone, spending my savings on Christmas Gifts. Christmas was the most magical time when Mary and Tom shopped for weeks, ready for Santa Claus to arrive. 'Has he been?' I would ask in the night, then always fall asleep and miss his arrival. Each year the pile of presents grew larger, but there was always a cardboard sweet shop, with little packets of sweets to put into boxes, and a post office with stamps and envelopes. The *Rupert Bear Book* and *Robin Annual* nestled in the pillowcase with toys that brought as much joy to my parents as to me.

***

In my ninth year, skipping down the dingy passage of 162, Mam and Dad broke the news. Mam was going to have another baby. What was this all about? Perhaps it would go away? But it certainly did not and I realised how happy my parents were when they were given the key to a new Police House on a council estate. This estate was a place for displaced families from the East End of town. Crime was rife, and some roads had pairs of police houses at each end, with occupants busy with local problems. I became accustomed to the frantic hammering on the door at night, and tried not to hear the loud and often drunken voices.

***

Our home was packed into boxes, and the windows whitewashed. I was moving away from my friends and familiar places, to one that was alien. But Mary and Tom were thrilled. The new house had three bedrooms, an inside toilet and a real bathroom. There were gardens at front and back, and a small green hill over the road. This meant a long bus trip and a fifteen-minute walk, twice a day to and back from school, as school dinners were never discussed. The bus fare must have eaten a hole in the small family income. Yet I was protected from this, travelling each day with my close friend Ruby who had also moved to the new estate. Ruby knew the ropes. We left the classroom ten minutes before the end of morning school every day, and in all weathers to catch the bus home for lunch. We walked together to Eden Vale, sometimes buying chips on the way, sometimes hiding in the large concrete pipes waiting to be sunk underground, or buying 'flying saucer' sweets or frozen 'Jubblies' from Butes on the corner. The days were endless, and summers eternal.

Jill

There was mud everywhere the winter that Jill was born. The pavements were unmade and the roads unfinished. The number 3 bus had its terminus just around the corner from 218 Allendale Road. This was a long ride from town and Dad began to worry about how far he might be away when Mam needed him. I would often come back late from school, wandering with my friends, doing nothing in particular but chatting with other young girls, like fledglings preparing to fly. Looking back, it was as if I had suddenly been pushed out of the nest to make way for the new baby. This was the beginning of my independence. Tom found a pram and a cot from adverts in the *Echo*, and cleaned and polished them.

On fifth February 1957, Dad hurried me to the door and ran with me to catch the next bus. I had walked up Chester Road with my friend Ruby and waited while she had her weekly elocution lesson so I was late home. Lots of children were sent to elocution in the early 50s. Mary was in the General Hospital in Chester Road, but Dad did not tell me what was happening, and we jumped off the bus at Barnes Park and into a red telephone box. 'It's a girl' Dad said. Even then I didn't realise what was happening. We skipped and ran the mile or so along Cleveland Road to the hospital. In later years, as I watched him struggling with breathing, I would remember his agility the night that Jill was born.

Mary stayed in hospital for a week, as all new mothers living in towns did in those days. She came home to the newly decorated spare bedroom where she rested for many more days, nursing her baby. Mary was almost forty, much older than was advised for motherhood then. Dad helped as much as he could and would often got Jill off to school when she was old enough. We worked together. I enjoyed polishing the shoes while Dad made breakfast, a pattern that would last for years. The house was cold in the mornings and I would find my socks on top of the oil heater, warming. Just one of the many thoughtful ways that Tom wrapped a safety cloud around his children. So my independence grew and I was I was secure—deeply loved and cared for by mam and dad. Later Mary and Tom revelled in the role of grandparent and the grandchildren simply adored them.

Jill brought joy to her parents. I took her for long walks in her pram and helped Tom clean up the latest batch of second hand toys. Mam bought a beautiful grey silk evening dress for the police ball. I was left to care for Jill, but had little idea of how to calm this crying baby. I worked out a plan. I would pretend to be Mam. It didn't work. I was ten but things were different then. In many ways they mirrored what I found in Northern Ghana fifty years later. Small children took care of smaller ones. They did a better job than me.

The summer that I was ten, I joined the Guides at Bishopwearmouth Church (later promoted to Sunderland Minster) with my friends Ruby and Janice. I was in the White Rose Patrol and Captain Laura Millbanke talked about camp and latrines. I could go to camp, couldn't I? I had never spent a night away from my parents, so I planned to make a corner of the tent my own, where I would be safe. But I had tummy ache, and Captain Laura decided that I was constipated and should use the latrines, whatever they were. Then she asked me to peel potatoes. Total shock! After three days, I was taken home, transported in a car belonging to a second homesick guide. We stopped on the way and ate banana sandwiches then, at home, Dad bundled me onto his knee while I cried with relief. I would never have believed that this frightened young girl guide would grow the confidence and determination needed to make it possible to undertake travel alone to some incredibly difficult places. Northern Ghana took top prize for that, beating even Kosovo.

I knew that we never had money to spare. It did not worry me at all.

'Do you want a cornet pet? You can, but we will have to walk home. We haven't enough money for the bus fare and an ice cream.' I felt guilty for even thinking about such a treat and so we caught the bus.

There was the day when I was six when some visitors called to the house in Chester road, in a car! They had darkened skin and were talking about a holiday and going in an aeroplane. I didn't know what a holiday was and had never seen a plane except in Rupert Books. The man gave me a sixpence all for myself! I sometimes had sixpence to take to school to buy saving stamps. Some of these had Prince Charles' photo on them, others Princess Anne's. I had a special purse to take money to school in and bring the stamps home then mam would help me to stick them in the flimsy book. I was, of course, oblivious to what happened next—almost as regularly mam took the book to the Post Office to reclaim the money back so that I could buy more the next week.

Mary often made 'toffee cakes' for my friends and me. These were simply sugar and margarine with a little vinegar, all boiled up in an old pan. The secret of knowing when toffee had been made was to drop some of the thickening syrup into cold water. If it set into an elastic rope, it was ready. Then the toffee was poured into well-greased cake-tins that held twelve toffee-cakes. Sometimes, when the children had collected enough old iced-lolly sticks from the gutters, mam would wash them and stick one into a toffee cake so it could be eaten like a lolly. Perfect recipe for building resistance to disease. Not wonderful for teeth.

Later, fully grown and remarkably independent from the time my sister appeared on the scene, I wanted to do something about the lack of money. Mam and dad were kind. They let me buy comics and go to the cinema. But I wanted to buy my own presents for family and friends at Christmas. And I wanted to buy records for my treasured Dansette. This was the second family record player—the first was a wind-up that scraped its way around the grooves of the old 78s. Needles had to be changed constantly and the family were so proud. This record player arrived at about the same time as the television set—rented, small and wonderful. Having our own television had been a dream. One of the families living in Chester Road had a tiny TV. Once I watched 'Muffin the Mule' Such an adventure. When we moved to the Police House on the council estate, my parents became friends with a kind family who lived in a very smart house a field away from Farringdon. They owned a leather shop in town, kept horses and had a cleaning lady as well as a television. The Luccock family would go there together to watch 'Nicholas Nickelby' on Sunday evening. So, having our own TV was momentous.

Dad promised to find out about Saturday jobs in town. I read the adverts I the local paper 'The Echo'. Then it would have been impossible to believe that, one day, the Echo would travel to Africa with me. The advert read

'Wanted. Saturday assistant. Sunderland Jewellery Shop'

So I called in. They had no telephone. The young manager explained that they needed Saturday help until Christmas. The pay was £1 a day. I said 'yes please' This was my first and most tedious job. The staff room was part of an under-stairs corridor but there was a toilet. I stood around and stood around each Saturday in the weeks before Christmas. I did make sales—an odd powder compact or clock. Clocks were a nightmare. Their boxes lived upstairs, in a heap on the floor. So, if one was sold, the whole large heap had to be explored. I really didn't like selling rings either. When blushing brides-to-be found one to try on, all was fine until they the ring became stuck. This happened again and again. The manager put a notice in the window advertising 'ear piercing'. The first time he tried this, the ear bled so much that an ambulance was needed. This, of course, meant that I would never have pierced ears. And it was something I remembered as I learned of and saw the tremendously significant and detailed tribal markings of my future African friends. I was asked me in disbelief if it was true that white people had rings in their eyebrows and noses.

After that, much to the horror of our grammar school headmistress, I always found work. Saturdays at British Home Stores were long days. At that time, each department was laid out on counters in an oblong shape. The assistants stood in the middle of this. Trapped. She was put on the lighting counter. Every light-bulb had to be tested before it was sold. At first, they just broke in my hand as I tried to push them into the test socket, sending a shower of fine glass across the other lamp-shades and sockets. Later I was sent to run the record department. This was much better, spread along a side wall. Getting paid to play the newest records was a dream job.

Later, working in a record shop seemed even more exciting. The walk to work took half an hour. I walked everywhere. The inexperienced young shop owner wanted me there so he could celebrate the Sabbath. He had thought that they would be very busy on Saturdays. After a few weeks of the slowest of trade, I had worked my way through all the '45s and moved on to the LPs. and was relieved when her boss first cut her time to half days then decided to close down. I tried Notarriani's Italian Ice cream parlour in the High Street. The full-time girls and women made mince-meat of me. I had no real experience of such loud, confident, behaviour. Their experiences were too different, they didn't like me. I was too 'posh' so my work was emptying and cleaning ash trays. I dropped a heavy tray of glass sundae dishes down a staircase and lasted a day.

Being an usherette at The Ritz cinema brought a dull brown uniform, a torch and a tray of ice creams and drinks to carry up and down the aisles. The Ritz had been my favourite Saturday Morning cinema. With my friends Edward and Peter, I stood in the long queue waiting for opening time. We sang songs, then watched cartoons, a cowboy film, then a serial. These were deliriously happy days.

Standing at the back of the smoke-filled room as an usherette, watching and re-watching the same film, was not so good. On the fourth day I left, probably to the joy of my headmistress who often called me in to tell me she would never succeed at school if I worked on Saturdays.

Summer holidays were different. Never happier than when by the sea, I applied for a job at 'Alfredos' on the sea front. They needed a shop assistant for the summer. My new boss and his wife were kindness itself and worked themselves to exhaustion on the shop and café behind. I began working for five pounds for six days a week. The owners quickly decided that they wanted me to stay and raised my pay by a pound at the end of the first week.

The shop part was in front of the café that served fish and chips and pie and chips to the large numbers of day-trippers who came to Seaburn, often by bus. The shop sold basic things like bread, tins of soup, biscuits, but the main summer trade was buckets and spades, windmills, candy rock. There were jars of sweets and tiger nuts. Each morning I filled the tiger nut jar from a large Hessian sack in the garage behind the shop. There must have been mice. The yard was used to hold dustbins full of peeled potatoes for the large volumes of chips fried every day, peeled by 'Etta, a short, rounded, bouncy lady who did her best to keep staff cheery through constant stories and much laughter. 'Mr Alfredo' himself was also short and rotund, always splendid in his plus fours. I had never encountered plus fours, but they seemed natural attire for my boss. He treated his staff well and they worked hard. I would sing as I cleaned the large plate glass windows or the toilet. At 'dinner time' I crossed the road to sit on the sandy beach or the concrete benches that edged the promenade. In bad weather, I sat in the large white shelter and watched the wildness of the sea. On these days the shop was quieter. So there was too much bread. I was shown how to soften the bread by punching the loaves so that customers would think it was fresh. These were the days before 'sell by' dates.

'Mrs Alfredo' greeted customers enthusiastically, particularly the locals. Everyone was welcome, even the dogs. Her height and careful grooming gave her authority that seemed to transmit itself to day-tripping children who were always well behaved in her shop.

Each summer I came back to Alfredo's. In my Uni summers, I walked from there to my night job at 'The Rink.' This had been the ice rink in Park Lane in the centre of Sunderland It was converted into a large dance hall, with a stage and lots of room. In the sixties it was the place to be seen. The resident band supported the many visiting hopeful young music groups. Many of these had short-lived fame, but some went on to become real stars.

The advert in the Sunderland Echo for a 'relief cashier' at the dance hall was too good to miss. The manager who interviewed me clearly wanted at least to employ me. Later I often regretted turning down his suggestion that I might want to be a Disc Jockey. This was the job I would have done without pay. Cashiering –in the kiosk near the entrance, was well paid but lonely. In those days, everything was cash. On Saturday nights the Rink attracted hundreds and takings soared. I worked late, counting the piles of notes they had stacked around the manager's office.

I preferred working in the dance hall itself. There was a kiosk storing handbags so that girls did not have to put them on the floor and dance round them. Another was the cloakroom. There was a popular burger stall and an even more poplar bar. I enjoyed working in all of these, liking the company of the other staff, talking to the customers and being close to the music. I liked the guitarist in the resident band and was flattered by his shy friendship.

When the Rink closed at night, most staff moved on to one of the new night-clubs where they stayed very late. They were allowed to charge management for taxis as no buses worked after closing time. I preferred to get home, particularly as I had to be up early for my 'day job'. During the Christmas holidays I combined the Rink with a post round, so was totally occupied. The Rink was particularly busy.

At Christmas, on the post, I worked on my home round, with Ronnie, the kind postman who had worked on Leechmere Road for many years. He showed me how to load up my bag at the town sorting office twice every day, taking the bus to and from the round. The bag was heavy, the paths to the houses steep and difficult in the snow and frost of 60s winters. Fifty years later, by chance, I recognised Ronnie walking at the sea-front in Sunderland and this lovely man remembered me, my family and even my home address. Love and life inevitably took me too far away but I always returned.

Even while at Leicester, learning to teach chemistry, I needed to work. Times were hard for Tom and Mary and they could not help as much as they would have liked, but really I thought nothing of selling potatoes from door to door around the council estates near Scraptoft or working six nights a week behind a bar. My longest days were taken up by cleaning the central Leicester beauty parlour early in the morning where I became the receptionist during the day before walking to the local pub to serve drinks. I would sometimes hitch-hike back to Sunderland, unaware of any danger. Sometimes I went to lectures but not too often, particularly if the sun shone. I was sent to Suffolk to practise my science teaching. There I met, and later married, Roger, a farm manager. We moved to Norfolk, had two daughters and my way of life here bore no recognition to that in Sunderland. In many ways it was perfect.

Chapter Seven
Going to Northern Ghana

My first visit to Ghana, indeed to Africa, in 1995 was funded by a charity set up to improve science education in the developing world. My friendship with Karimu had grown, although I felt uncomfortable when he told me that he was sure that my visit was one of the most important things that had ever happened to him. I had learned so much from his letters, and began to feel privileged to have such a rich source of information from someone who deeply cared for and understood his homeland. His letters were on thin air-mail paper in the neatest of hand-writing, always many pages long. He tried so hard to explain about the country he loved so much and desperately wanted to help.

An early letter, in 1994 told me:

The South of Ghana has a better climate than the North, rain almost all the year round with two peaks. In the North there is one rainy season and a long, dry, hot season. Soils are rich in the South and support all the economic crops like cocoa, rubber, fruits, sugar cane and kola nuts. The North has no exportable crop, only shea nuts. The people are mostly subsistence farmers and can hardly produce enough for their family. In Wulugu people begin to starve after Christmas. What is worse is that education is failing in the North. Many parents are not able to pay school fees.

His passion for helping Northerners overcome the difficulties that kept them in the poverty that most were resigned to became an obsession. He was deeply Christian, and felt it was God's will that he should work to improve lives for his people. His letters revealed a panorama of every-day life that was rooted in ancient beliefs and tribal loyalties.

Although communicating in this way slowed everything down, I always felt privileged to read Karimu's accounts of life in Ghana written in his own hand. Eventually they would be replaced by e-mail.

On my first visit to Ghana, my first tentative step into Africa, I travelled with a colleague who often reminded me of his extensive experience in this massive continent. He had no doubts about his depth of knowledge. I had no doubts about my ignorance. I had been warned about Kotoka airport in Accra, that there would be crowds fighting to carry my bags, even carry me, for a price! I knew that I had to watch everything closely and that I was a target for thieves. Complete mayhem in the luggage hall in stifling heat made clear thinking impossible. Somehow, in the steaming heat and deafening babble, we found our luggage and were pushed along by heaving masses to reach the exit where crowds were being controlled with whips. Then I heard 'Lynne, over here, over here.' In the sea of faces in the darkness of the African night, where lighting was poor, I tried to follow the voice. Then someone took my trolley. I was sure I'd been robbed although by then I was past caring. I just needed to escape from the crush of people. Then, to my overwhelming relief, I found Karimu at my side, saying, 'OK, this way, we have a truck.'

As we reached the very smart vehicle, so did the luggage. A miracle. 'This is Joseph,' said Karimu introducing the young 'luggage thief.' He will travel with us.' We climbed in, inching our way slowly through the crowds and the traffic. 'Tonight you will stay at the university,' said Karimu. 'Professor Nabila has loaned us his vehicle.' Joseph became a firm friend. We were able to help the school in Kpasenkpe where he taught, with desks and, much later, computers. He was part of the very large family of Chief John Nabila, who was hoping that I would want to help more with education projects.

Historically, Northerners had lost out in the education stakes. It was commonly said that, during Colonial times, the British felt that the South should be educated, but the Northerners were savages, only fit for manual work. The damage of that legacy is apparent today. Travel to and through the North is fraught with danger. Roads, where they exist, are poor. Electricity reaches the larger settlements most of the time but vast areas of land are so remote it is doubtful that they will ever be connected to the grid. Solar power is only a partial solution, requiring servicing from engineers who will not go there. In 1995, most children had left school by fourteen, with most girls not going to school at all. In this polygamous society, each husband had at least three wives, each wife producing a baby most years. A wife's role was to feed the husband, the Supreme Being in their compound of round mud-huts. The world stretched as far as Tamale or Bolgatanga. There were no newspapers, no television or radio in villages without electricity. News spread slowly, as did life with its predetermined rhythm of night and day, flood and famine, birth and death. The children had no manufactured toys, no books, paper or pencils. They played with whatever they found, drawing in the dust using a stick or a stone. They sang, played music on primitive drums, bells and whistles. They washed when there was water, and were usually clean. The mothers made soap from wood ash from the fire and palm oil, and wore pieces of colourful cloth until they disintegrated. Rags and straw were used for nappies. They breast-fed their babies, and any-one else's when necessary. If a mother was too sick to produce milk, another would step in. That way, if they survived, most babies were healthy before weaning. Traditionally, a new born was kept inside the hut for its first week, until 'outdooring' when the father would carry the baby out and hold it up for the gods to bless. Many babies did not survive the first week and were quietly buried by their mothers, who were simply expected to move on; understanding that it was the will of whichever god the family worshiped.

Belief in a god simplified life, but did not lessen the pain. Villagers had an acceptance of events as god's will. Many had moved from traditional gods to Islam, and some had been reached by Christian missionaries. I was to discover that, in every primary school, The Lord's Prayer was said each day in English, another colonial legacy that made no sense to most. These children would walk as far as five miles without shoes to school. They would clean and sweep, and listen closely to the teacher. If the teacher was absent, they waited all day with their prefect in charge, using his cane when necessary. None of these schools had toilets, so children squatted anywhere. If they needed to wipe themselves, they would search for a scrap of paper, a few leaves or a handful of soil. Teachers just had to manage. Sometimes they had to bicycle to a piece of land with some shade, increasingly hard as more and more trees were cut for charcoal.

Widespread belief that menstrual blood was dirty meant that girls were kept at home during their periods. Lack of access to any sanitary protection meant that they used the oldest of rags and washed them; simple in the rainy season, not so in the drought. There was also the tradition for Muslim girls to marry as soon as they first menstruated, even if they had been in school, meaning that their chance to learn and so to move out of poverty was removed forever.

I did not realise in the early days that our involvement might be far more effective had we improved hygiene through the provision of toilets, thus playing a key role in keeping girls in school. But the problem was complex. Toilets would need cleaning. As a science teacher, I had developed a deep interest in the teaching of science that would improve lives across the world. In my own school I enjoyed introducing new courses that actually put this into practice, alongside the more traditional curriculum. Internationally I was privileged to work with practising science teachers, deciding together what could be introduced into science lessons that would be both useful in terms of making lives better and interesting enough so that children would begin to absorb this and use it when needed.

Karimu and I had decided to encourage our girl students to write to each other, so opening up another way to foster real understanding and interest in science. I found much of the UK's chemistry curriculum dry, meaningless and irrelevant in today's society. But very soon, the letters from the Wulugu girls brought a breath of fresh air into chemistry lessons in Norfolk. Reading about the breakdown of a village Shea butter extraction machine because of rust made my students really want to understand how this had happened, and how to stop a recurrence. The mind-numbing chemistry of rusting, with the obligatory blast furnace diagrams, became exciting. The syllabus section on insecticides and pollution took on new meaning when my students learned about it from the perspective of a 16-year old Wulugu girl, who explained that the DDT crop insecticide, was sometimes used by girls to commit suicide to avoid marriage to an old man. These marriages were often arranged at birth, and there was no way out except to drink the deadly chemical, long since banned in most of Europe.

This pre-determined early marriage pathway for girls was usually inescapable. I saw this clearly during my early years of working with Ghanaian communities. At one meeting of school head-teachers, the conversation seamlessly moved from witches to weddings. One headmaster sadly spoke of his thirteen-year-old daughter who had recently married. He turned to me, looked into my ignorantly critical gaze, and said, 'what could I do? My family are hungry, I got three cows for my daughter.'

If this was happening even in the more educated families, there were mountains to climb if anything was to change for the masses whose lives were governed by abject poverty. The reality is often different from what is immediately perceived. In the years that followed, I learned that teachers, particularly in the North, were very poorly paid, and often not at all for months. Head-teachers sometimes tried to help, but their income was not large. To make matters worse, the head always took the blame for a badly functioning school. When pupils were unhappy with their school, they have been known to take the law into their own hands. One of the heads at this same meeting had his house burned down by angry students. While there were few girls attending schools in the North, there were equally few women teachers to act as role models. For a woman to teach here, she needed accommodation. Sometimes the village chief offered them a room. Chiefs have many wives and assumed that any woman would be honoured to be among them. So female teachers' stays were short, they simply ran away and could not be replaced.

Our fledgling charity, 'The Wulugu Project,' saw that one of the solutions to the problem of lack of women teachers was to provide hostels for them. It was difficult to persuade donors that this was a good idea, but eventually

Wulugu schools were accompanied by teacher blocks whenever the money could be raised. Here the teachers were safe, living happily near their school, even being allowed to bring their husbands. But nothing is ever straightforward. The sheer remoteness of some schools from the towns meant that all teachers needed somewhere to live and this was a tall order.

Without accommodation the one to two-hour journey would be one of the many causes of frequent teacher absences. Children also had reasons for being out of school. They often lived miles away as there were not enough local schools. Girls' mothers needed them at home to care for younger siblings or to help grow food, and to sometimes sit by the road holding a basket of mangos, then leaping up and waving at anyone who passed by. Sometimes they would be sent to customs points where lorries and cars were forced to stop. This was a better way to sell, but many others had the same idea. For older girls, this trade was perilous and has been blamed for the spread of diseases, including HIV.

Karimu found that, in one village, the women there were doing what they could to make lives better. They met each week, bringing small amounts of money collected by the leader of the group. Months later the amount was enough to fund one woman to set up a small local enterprise. After a year, she was to repay with ten per cent interest. Talking to the women about their hopes for their children's education, Karimu suggested they could help their girls attend school if the other women had loans. The group leapt on the idea. None of them had ever been to school, yet they knew that school meant a better future. The project's *loans for women* began. Other charities were already operating loan schemes, but not in the deprived Wulugu districts. We did our best to find out how these schemes operated. Mostly, loans were administered by committee, and controlled by a computer programme. Wulugu loans were run by people from the district who understood the particular needs of each family. There were no computers. The women themselves decided who should receive what, taking into account individual circumstances. I was heartbroken by official refusals to fund loans for 'our' villages as they insisted on outside monitoring and use of the required computer programme. But I had proof that this was often unhelpful, that the women could be trusted to organise themselves although they were clear that they were accountable to each other and to the Wulugu Project team. Our Wulugu volunteers in Ghana were, and are, unique. They seem to be able to understand the real needs and the day-to-day problems, and earn the trust and co-operation of those who need their help. Local villagers see that they are completely different from other charity workers, they receive no payment except that they see that lives are becoming better for so many of the very poorest.

On this, my first venture into Ghana, Karimu and his colleagues treated me kindly, but often found my bewilderment amusing. It was probably very funny indeed as I was about as naïve as it is possible to be. We made this first journey north slowly, breaking me in gently. I was taken to the relatively affluent Cape Coast to visit Takoradi Girls' School, where Theresa worked. Theresa was the other Ghanaian friend I had met in Japan. She had encouraged the selection of Karimu for the trip. A wise lady, she knew of Karimu's problems in the North, and wanted to help. She proudly showed us her school, warning that it would not be the same everywhere, and thoughtfully gave me a cotton dress and a large fruitcake. 'You may need these.'

The lizards here were the largest so far. In even this smart the school library, books were being gradually destroyed by bugs. Further up the coast we were shown the slave caves in Elmina castle. This was the loading bay for the constant stream of ships from countries across the world, coming to collect their next batch of slaves.

Following a five hour drive, past thin beggars, thinner beasts and thousands of goats, we spent a night at a gold mine in the Ashanti Region, where the miners were enthusiastically drinking beer and celebrating 'Chuck Lotto.' The affluent Australian mine-owners held events like this as part of their welfare package. The prize for the free draw was a caged chicken. Not much of a prize perhaps but the miners seemed frenzied as they waited to hear who had won. This was clearly a big event. The wives of the management, who lived a privileged but difficult life, watched. The 'best band in Ghana'—The Golden Nuggets—were meant to be playing tonight. They didn't turn up. I soon learned that it would have been more of a surprise if things had worked as expected. Life in Ghana was unpredictable and certainly rarely ran according to plans.

The faces of these miners were as black as those of the Sunderland coal miners travelling home from work on the double decker buses, exhausted, thirsty and hungry.

For the Sunderland miners, this was their destiny, as that of their fathers and their fathers' fathers. They would always be poor but had somewhere to live and free coal for the fire. Most would die from damaged lungs.

The following morning, in the gold mine, I was laughingly invited to lift a gold bar, a surreal experience. I discovered that the workers had all left their villages and their small farms to seek wealth here. They were given bland, concrete houses with a school for the children. Their water and air were contaminated with arsenic and other toxins and many children had severe skin conditions. Hilltops were bare and black, something to do with the arsenic contaminating the water. Some hill-tops in Sunderland were bare and black at that time too; green hills full of life replaced by sterile slag heaps.

There were so many parallels with the Sunderland pitmen.

The gold mine managers were housed in large homes up-wind, with houseboys, hairdressers and gardeners. They had a swimming pool and a bakery. Food was imported for them and there was a good school. It seemed to me that some people were prospering here, but certainly not the Ashanti people. And little was spent on health. A quarter of a century later I talked with a medic working in Accra, the capital of Ghana. She told me that her father was a doctor at the same mine at the time I visited. It was good to learn that attempts even then were being made to maintain health of the workers. But she showed me her permanently damaged skin, caused by the contaminated air and water. The families of Sunderland miners breathed in the coal dust, it was inescapable. Any damage to their children's lives was probably restricted to the lungs.

As we moved North, things became more challenging. Kumasi, the second city in Ghana was popular with tourists. There is a very good science-based university here.

Further North, in Kintampo, when I needed a toilet, we tried the maternity hospital. The dirt and stench were too much. I couldn't go anywhere near it, and my bladder control suddenly improved. The last hotel en route was in the city of Tamale. It was dark, hot and fly-ridden; signs of what lay ahead. The caged doors of the sparse rooms reminded me of a prison. They were probably an attempt to keep out intruders.

Three long hours North of Tamale on a disastrous road we finally arrived at Wulugu School. I stayed in the 2-bedroom house that Karimu had built in the hope that he would attract international volunteers. There was a long-drop toilet, and I didn't realise what a privilege this was. Here I could sit watching a praying mantis at work. There was a cook, Ben,,an ex-boxer who had worked for the Britsh in Colonial times. He spoke good English and did his very best, serving spaghetti with pasteurised cheese slices painstakingly cut into tiny squares. Cheese was a rare luxury. On arrival, I was greeted by a message written in large stones on the ground. *Welcome Mrs Lynne Symonds.*

I had a piece of foam to sleep on the rough concrete floor. There was a ceiling fan. The temperatures were unbearable. My bed routine consisted of soaking my mattress and lying under a dripping towel. From here I was taken to see the reality of the deprivation in Wulugu, The Wulugu students sang to me and were delighted to have a white woman staying. They constantly peered into the non-curtained windows and stood patiently outside, waiting for a smile or a word.

Karimu had done his best to prepare me for life in the North. He had told me:

'Wulugu is a typical African village with a population of about three thousand. The people are subsistence farmers who are hardly able to feed their families. Wild vegetables help a lot during the rainy season. Houses are mud structures with thatched roofs, and students always complain of leaking roofs. The villagers don't get the right type of grass and they don't seem to have the right expertise for roofing. A few huts have zinc roofs. The only blockhouses are those found in my school: four classroom blocks, a library and a workshop. My teachers are eighteen in number, and so far I am the only one decently accommodated. The rest live in village mud huts. We had plans to build detached mud houses for our teachers in the dry season, and the villagers had agreed to do this for us.'

Nine years later, in 2004, when the population of the school was greatly increased, Karimu wrote;

There are 417 students, with 160 girls. Their courses are designed to lead them to university. The school took part in the Senior Secondary Certificate Examination last year. At this time the results in the whole country were disastrous. My school did well despite our difficult life here. Five out of fifty six qualified for university. They were the pioneer group who had textbooks designed for the courses that didn't have clear syllabuses. The result was mass failure, which prompted the government to re-register all last-year's candidates for this year.

This setback was overcome, as were most, and 'Wulugu Sec' continued as the most successful in the District. A testimony to the Head-teacher's determination.

Chapter Eight
On First Meeting the Chief, Spring 1995

The Mamprusi Kingdom of Ghana was founded, around the 16th century, by the Great Naa Gbanwah-Gbewah, at Pusiga, a village fourteen kilometers from Bawku. The Kingdom spans most of the Northern and the Upper East Regions of Ghana, and into Burkina Faso. As a consequence, the King of Mossi in Burkina is to this day enskinned by the Nayiri, the king of the Mamprugu, a tribe of a million people, establishing this kingdom as the only one in present-day Ghana whose relevance and authority cuts across national boundaries. The ethnicity is Mamprusi, and the language Mampruli. The Mamprusi were and are strong and proud. Harsh conditions bred a people equipped to deal with disease, famine and punishing weather. There were always many layers of chieftaincy, almost all occupied by men. But Queen Mothers were respected and revered, and they too had influence over the lives of the villagers. In those days, civil law helped maintain peace and make sure that everyone knew their place. Chiefs were expected to make wise rulings on local matters, receiving gifts from their people in return for advice and land. The Nayiri (Paramount Chief) had a throne made from leather cushions sitting on animal skins; leopard, antelope and lion, from the days when there were many wild creatures to hunt with spears and knives. He had a linguist who sat with the elders on the ground, everyone with their head below that of the esteemed and feared chief.

His 'Spearman' protected him.

I had much to learn about tribal traditions and the roles of chiefs and sub-chiefs. There were hushed accounts of what men would do to gain the title of Chief. Where there were a number of candidates, the time before the decision was one of great danger for them. Death by poisoning was not uncommon, so some became thin and gaunt, fearing the intervention of their rivals. Long established chiefs joked about their sedentary role. They marvelled that they had not become fat, even though they were not allowed to eat or drink in public. Chiefs must always walk slowly, in stately parade. They sit for long hours to greet and help their people. While visitors must bring a gift (money being the favourite) the chief was expected equally to help those in trouble who lacked food and resources.

Chiefs in the North are given their official role through a complex 'enskinment' ceremony when they are given animal skins that grow in numbers over the years into a sumptuous throne. This tradition came from the days when there were many wild animals to hunt with spears and machetes. Further south, chiefs were 'enstooled', the ceremony centring on a throne made from wood or even gold. But in the North resources were few. I was greatly honoured to be invited to meet the Paramount Chief of the Maprusi Tribe.

***

Approaching the mud hut palace, with my entourage of locals who took such care of me, I could hear the drums beating, announcing my arrival. I was shown to a bench under an acacia tree and told to wait in the forty-degree heat, my head foggy with tiredness, yet the flow of rich experiences a constant stimulation. There was, as always, everywhere, a long wait. Minutes passed slowly. Goats and guinea fowl scrabbled noisily in the dirt. The sun beat down with a wild ferocity that made everyone seek the shade. I was beckoned towards the dark opening to the palace and told to take off my sandals. Then I was led into the darkness and towards a long low bench facing the chief. My eyes adjusted to the darkness and my ears to the hushed and reverent tones that reminded me of being back home in church. The linguist began to speak slowly and loudly, his Mampruli words being translated, in hushed tones, into English by one of the elders.

'The white woman is welcome here. We, the Mamprusi people of West Mamprugu, are glad of the great assistance that you have given to our children in their schools. But we want you to do more. For too long we have been neglected by our leaders in Accra. Now we seek to give this generation the education they need to move out of the poverty that was brought by their forefathers. We ask you to return to London with this message and to find others to assist us in our battle.'

I replied,

'Thank you for allowing me to visit your land. I have grown to respect your people and to feel part of the

Mamprugu family. You should know that I am not a rich lady but will do what I can to persuade others to work with me to improve your lives.'

Then came the cola ceremony, just like Holy Communion I thought. A large metal teapot-type vessel was brought out. Something, I couldn't see what, was placed reverently inside. The pot was swirled to the left and right then brought towards me, a spindly, gnarled black hand pulling out something that looked like a brown shiny chestnut. 'Take it,' I was told. 'Now bite into it and chew.' The taste was bitter and I wanted to spit it out, but I had no choice, fifty pairs of eyes were watching. I managed to swallow a little, and hide the rest in my hand. I later found out that this cola nut sharing ceremony was a great honour. These nuts are a stimulant used to defeat fatigue. Drivers often use them.

A goat on a rope was pulled reluctantly towards me. 'Take it,' the voice instructed again. So I reached out and grasped the muddy rope, recognising that this was a generous gift but wondering what I would do with it when they left. We were directed to the doorway and out of the palace. The drumming became louder as I walked back to the truck. The intolerable heat in the palace had made sweat run down from my head to my feet. The dust was clinging to it, so my skin was red and damp. My dress stuck to my body. The goat was trussed and room found for it in the back of the truck. I was grateful now for the privilege of travelling in the front and I climbed up wearily, ready for the two hour journey along the dust tracks and dried river beds back to Wulugu.

Chapter Nine
The Invitation

Back in U.K. in the autumn of 1995, a letter arrived saying that the Nayiri, the most important Mamprusi Chief, had decided to enskin me to show me how much he appreciated my help, and to adopt me fully into the tribe. I was shocked, surprised and concerned, writing back to refuse. A white woman from Sunderland had no place being a chief of the Mamprusi. The biggest honour I had ever had to date was probably being a school prefect.

The world will know what you have done. Others will want to help too, he wrote.

'No,' I replied.

But if you accept, it will help us.

A year later, 1996, I was travelling back to Ghana, to be enskinned as the only white woman chief of a whole tribe in the North. I was told that I was the first white woman to be honoured in this way. I discovered that (in the South particularly) some white people, mainly from the USA, had bought themselves titles of smaller chiefs or been honoured with a village chieftaincy. Still I refused, until there came some reasoned pressure, based on the sheer deprivation of the region and lack of any attention from the government. The During the weeks before the trip to Ghana to be enskinned, came my first encounter with the press. Somehow the story was 'leaked,' and I was bombarded with requests for interviews, even woken by the phone in the middle of the night, live on air, to talk to BBC News. I had to learn how to handle the media very quickly.

Attention was focussed on my school life, a much-needed opportunity for good publicity for my school in Norfolk as well as for Wulugu School. There were offers of contracts, invitations to appear on national chat shows, and prime coverage by every English newspaper. My school students loved it all and learned a great deal. They were totally involved and even took part in interviews for TV and radio.

I had a request from *The Times* to send a photographer/ journalist to cover the ceremony for the front pages. Sky TV also announced that they would film it. I became concerned, as I did not want the attention to affect my relationships with the communities in Ghana. Talking it through with another influential chief, we agreed to allow one journalist only, to borrow a SKY camera but not to have TV journalists present. This was not easy to manage. A bright young *Times* photographer came with a reporter to photograph and interview me at work. Simon the photographer told me about some of the challenging stories he had covered in war zones, and did not anticipate any travel difficulties.

Just we were due to travel, a second national newspaper announced that they would send a reporter. I politely explained that there was to be only one, but was told that I could not stop them. Without local cooperation however, no one could reach the village where the enskinnment was to take place. I imagined at this point that I had learned to handle the press, but was continually disappointed by the subsequent untruths and exaggerations. Meanwhile, back in Ghana, Karimu was planning. I did not know about the skilful and essential negotiations that made sure that everyone important was properly consulted. My enskinnment would be unique. There were a few wealthy visitors who'd been given a chief's name by the chief of a village they had helped, but I was to be honoured with a whole tribal chieftaincy.

This major enskinnment was clearly the decision of the Nayiri, the Paramount Chief of the Mamprusi. He was illiterate, wise, elderly and greatly respected. He also had many wives, as was expected of an important chief. Another high status and influential chief, the Wulugu Naba insisted that this was actually *his* duty. This man, wiser than his years, needed to help his beloved Mamprusi tribe move on from harmful traditions, yet keep the best of their way of life. He knew that it was time to reverse colonialism's legacy of poverty that prevented any more than basic education for these 'hostile' Northerners. It had become too easy for the hundreds of villages to keep their girls at home to help with the crops, sell in the market, or care for siblings. His arguments were forceful. I had formed a bond with the Mamprusi people, there was real friendship between us that ignored skin colour and made it possible for me to work with ordinary people to begin to change things for the better, where others, richer, more powerful, and certainly more experienced in African matters had failed. Quite a tall order! Aid agencies came and went, charities mushroomed, did what they thought was needed then disappeared, along with their impotent attempts, sometimes inadvertently harming those they had tried to help as they re-enforced the habit of sitting back and waiting for the 'white man who would provide.'

As a long-term mentor for Karimu, in university and beyond, Wulugu Naba, widely recognised as a truly wise professor, was sure that he was right. He had helped during my first visit to Ghana by providing a truck and his own driver, putting me up in the guest residences at Legon University in Accra, and hosting a dinner party for me. The enskinnment would be performed by him in his own village, Kpasenkpe. A second ceremony would happen in Wulugu. The following day, there would be yet another ceremony at Nalerigu, where the Paramount Chief, The Nayiri, had his palace.

We checked in at Heathrow. This was Roger, my husband's his first visit to Africa. Some time later, Simon appeared. The stop in Northern Nigeria took longer than expected, but we did eventually arrive at Kotoka airport in the early evening, where the queues and the heat increased the discomfort. There was a problem with the SKY News camera. Customs needed a deposit for this, and assured us that we could re-claim it when the camera left the country again. Everything took a very long time and there was pandemonium at the luggage belt. It was hot, dark and the smell of sweat was overpowering. There were so many people, mostly on their way home to Ghana, some travelling for two days from the USA via Heathrow.

Simon meanwhile was taking a taxi to an up-market hotel, telling our caretakers that he wouldn't travel north with them and had arranged to hire a car. Early next day Karimu arrived with a truck. The driver Sandow, who became such a good friend over the years, was one of the many who seemed to be at the beck and call of superiors and chiefs. The social divisions between rich and poor, high and low status were accompanied by meek subservience on the one hand and what I saw as rudeness on the other. That is how it still often is in many places, despite so-called progress. As we were loading for the first part of our journey, a taxi drew up. 'I'll have to come with you,' shouted Simon. 'The hire car thing didn't work.'

'OK, there is room,' Karimu told him, while grinning at me. The truck was new and very comfortable. Leaving Accra seemed to take hours. Traffic was just a mess and there were terrible potholes. The journey north took two days, the heat making things difficult. There were, of course, no roadside cafes and certainly no toilets. For me, the only female, things were far from easy. We stopped for much longer than seemed necessary in a village to buy chief's sandals. These had soles made from an old tyre and harsh plastic straps, ornately coloured with a yellow pom-pom. They were most inelegant, and I couldn't walk in them. 'That doesn't matter,' said Karimu, who often tried to persuade me that all was well. 'You won't be walking. They will carry you.'

local elders felt strongly that rewarding me with a chieftaincy would draw the attention of the world's media to their plight. They were right, of course.

Chapter Ten
Mamprusi Enskinnment

Wednesday 3rd April 1996. The relentless Meltemi wind blew the biting dust through the stark mud huts, turning clothes lava red and forcing the ragged rams to turn their backs against its anger. Guinea fowl scuttled and picked around in the dirt, while vultures circled hopefully overhead, their outlines ghostly, masked by the dust. But today was different. Cockerels crowed in the dawn, unheard as the drumming continued, ever louder, vibrating through every sinew as if trying to enter the bloodstream. Perhaps the men had danced through the long night, where the blistering heat made certain that no sleep could interfere with its unquestioned ownership of lives and land.

Today was the day of my enskinnment, a new Naa, honorary chief of the strong Mamprusi peoples would be welcomed. My title would be Neesim Poanaba. The feverish frenzy of the competing and unprincipled press and television news crews seemed to belong to another world, alien to what was going on. They wanted to be part of the bizarre, the tribal law - the *uncivilised*. How could they begin to understand that today would be a celebration of the triumphs of a tribe of fierce strength and pride, where the demands of daily survival had bred a race of men and women with minds sharper and clearer than those whose lives had been cushioned by Western medicine and guaranteed food and water.

I rose from under the crumpled covering on the rough piece of yellowed foam that had been prepared for the bed of a chief in waiting. It was sodden and stained from my vain attempts to cool my baking body with water from the bucket by my side. I was encrusted by a coating of desert grit, and throughout the night had been aware of the twenty bodies lying outside my small mud room, the sleeping Muslims who had woken to pray for their new chief and for the future of their hungry children. I needed to rise above my great exhaustion knowing that I must play my role with integrity and honour. To fail would be to insult the thousands who would celebrate the new hope that I had brought into their lives. I must be clean, must eat to avoid total exhaustion, must control the constant need to empty my guts, and be wise in my addresses to the gathering crowds. I had been carefully schooled in the rituals of chieftaincy, and knew that thousands of eyes would be on me today. But there would be no criticism, simply joy that I had, at last, agreed to become an essential part of this massive effort to break away from the hunger and needless suffering of recent generations.

Stepping carefully past the mounds of animal dung, avoiding the hidden snake holes, I tried to find a private place to start the day. As always, wherever I went, friendly faces peered at me with curiosity and sometimes excitement. The babies cried with terror as they saw what must have seemed like a monster in their brown eyes. I walked slowly to the back of the nearest mud house, part of a Kpasenkpe compound. In this beautiful village, as all over the northern region, compounds were formed from round houses with roofs that looked like parasols woven from local grass. Each block for the homes was made from local mud dried in the sun and put together with mathematical precision. The block structures were then covered with a smoothing layer of mud, and sometimes the rooms had wooden window and doorframes. There was no glass in the windows of course. There was a room for each wife and one for the husband, with a 'washroom' and sometimes a small grain store. The grain store was often empty as the weather in this region was so unkind. The round rooms were themselves built in a circle, surrounding a central yard. Here women cooked in giant pots over open fires, using wood they had carried on their heads for miles. The ever-approaching Sahara made sure that their journeys would become more arduous. Goats, sheep, chickens, cats and small children wandered freely. The only living things in any danger were the pigs. In this harshest of environments, where I marvelled at the harmony between all religious groups, the only sign of conflict came when pigs strayed in the path of Muslims and sometimes were slaughtered.

Making my way back to my temporary Kpasenkpe home, I remembered the reactions of Ghanaians I had met in England when they knew that I had friends in the North. They told me that the people of the North were fierce, that it was unsafe, that there were bloody tribal wars. They told me that it was far away, but nothing about the tortuous journey, as few had risked it. The drumming grew louder as the heat dried my throat. I washed with what precious water remained in my bucket, knowing there were long hours ahead.

Chapter Eleven
Neesim Poanaba

The crowds stretched away into the distance. Most had arrived early in the day to watch the enskinnment. Some had come by bicycle but most had walked for miles. The air heaved and shimmered with heat and anticipation. 'Come Chief, everything is ready' Karimu told me. This was the first time I had been called 'Chief.' 'Please put on the trousers,' he said. These were traditional woven trousers, part of my new robes. I stepped outside wearing a plain white cotton blouse and my new trousers. One of the children came to ask to help and was given my bag to guard. We walked slowly and solemnly to the durbar ground, where we greeted each of the dignitaries, shaking hands and smiling. Very few spoke English. This large group included many village chiefs and members of District Assemblies. From there, sitting on benches behind, we greeted the elders, then the many wives.

Across the dust, under burning sun, I was led to my seat with Karimu at my side. I held tightly on to my large bottle of water. Husband Roger was using the SKY TV camera to film everything. Simon the reporter couldn't believe his luck when his suggestion that they we needn't take our own photos, as he would be photographing everything, them his, was naively and trustingly accepted. 'You know I would give anything to change places with you,' he told me that morning.

The drumming quietened and everything became still. The sun was unrelenting as it watched over as Karimu formally introduced me to the crowds. The microphone was working for once. Wulugunaba stood up regally, holding his chief's stick. In Mampruli he welcomed the crowds and explained the order of things. Karimu translated for me. Then a tall, thin man dressed in his dancing smock walked over to me and said in English, 'It is time.'

The crowds erupted with excitement. The women made their unique warbling noise, 'ululation', used only at the most important occasions. Two women from Wulugu village, dressed in the most colourful clothes took their places behind me, using homemade straw fans to cool me as I walked to re-greet Chief Nabila and his entourage. Then to a pile of six brown and orange leather cushions on the red earth. Accompanying himself on a large talking drum, a singer sang about Karimu Nachia and his efforts to help his people. Then he sang about me, telling what had been achieved over the past three years.

Chief Nabila stood looking all-powerful. He announced the enskinnment. Two more women brought a pile of woven clothes. They were bright orange and black and heavy. The singer began again loudly as I was helped up to stand. The fan ladies stood behind, thrashing the air rapidly to lessen the heat. I was shown the smock, intricately embroidered with the symbols of chieftaincy. They held it over my head and paused while the vast crowds erupted again with jubilation as they lowered the large smock over my head. I tried to find the armholes but it was rapidly raised again and held above my head. As tradition dictates this was done three times, and on the last I was left wearing my beautiful chief's smock.

A strange hat made from the same material was presented next. Again it was put on my head three times before it was left in place. This hat reminded me of Robin Hood's. It was triangular, with a flap at each side held up by fasteners. The purpose of these was to cover my ears when I did not want to listen. A very straight staff, cut from local trees and covered in goatskin, was held out to me. The moment I accepted it, I became Chief of Mamprugu. The singer sang about me again. Chief Nabila announced my title 'Neesim Poanaba, Chief of Enlightenment and Education.'

Another wiry young man approached me and hoisted me onto his shoulders, still holding my Chief's stick. I think my attempts to look 'regal' fell apart then! It felt high and unstable. As my bearer carried me the crowds surrounded and followed, raising the dust so that we were enveloped in a red fog. The drummers drummed more loudly. We reached a large mud hut, the palace of the Kpasenkpe chief. Relieved to be back on the ground, the throne had arrived before me. Older chiefs also had animal skins to sit on as well as cushions. Dancers performed enthusiastically for me and to pay homage. There was a tradition of sticking cedi notes on the foreheads of dancers, as they always stuck to the perspiration. Things became quiet when a large group of Imams came to pray for me. A wooden tray loaded with bleeding animal parts was presented. This was the goat that had been sacrificed in my honour. The skin, once dried, would be this new chief's first skin and I would sit on it. Karimu appeared and told me that I must choose the goat parts I would eat, that they would be cooked for me. I pointed to the least bloody piece, certain that I would never eat it.

Exhausted and exhilarated, I was led back to the place where my bed waited. A simple generator lit a single fluorescent light bulb. There was a long drop toilet a short walk away, but the snake population made this hazardous after dark. My insides were virtually empty, and as any spare water in my body was lost through perspiration toilets weren't so essential. Outside the noise intensified, the party was in full swing with tens of thousands celebrating this first ever enskinnment of a white woman Mamprusi Chief. Roger and I rested while Simon constantly took photos.

'Your food is ready, a voice said. It was dark and a little cooler. The full moon was low in the sky, shining brightly, and there was my special sacrificial goat with mounds of joliff rice.

The three white guests ate together, too tired to talk. The day had been overwhelming. I listened. The drumming had stopped abruptly. The talking of the crowds sounded different now. Then I realised that the moon was disappearing. An eclipse. Everyone believed that the new chief caused this. At the point of total blackness there was absolute silence. As the night brightened again I saw the kind faces of Imams and elders who had gathered to protect me for the night. Now that really was an honour. I was beginning to feel more at ease with my title.

Partying continued in the village throughout the night. As we climbed into the truck to leave, more crowds seemed to come from no-where. They must have slept in the open. They all wanted to see their new chief. Children ran in front of the vehicle, running behind as it moved off, me waving from the window. This journey was to Wulugu where the second celebration was to take place.

We drove through parched and barren land. Any trees had long since been cut for fuel for stoves. Cattle were thin, the ponds dry. Lizards crouched under rocks or tried sheltering behind the termite hills. Constant bumping of the truck made me take off my seat belt as it repeatedly dug into my stomach. Then I kept hitting my head on the roof. The driver stopped suddenly. Perhaps he needed to relieve himself.

There was angry conversation in Mampruli, and then we realised we had a puncture. There was no village nearby, no other traffic, and mobile phones did not exist here. We climbed out into what felt like an oven of overpowering heat. There was no shelter. It was at times like this that I understood why thick clothes are important. I was wearing a white shirt and my ubiquitous straw hat that used to be white. Now it was a strange shade of red because of the dust that permeated everything. I walked to a skeleton of a tree trying to escape the heat. But I soon felt unwell. It took only thirty minutes to fix the puncture, but that was too long in almost fifty degrees.

We drove on to Wulugu where crowds were already celebrating. We stopped at the Voluntary Service Overseas teachers' house where I lay on the floor shivering with heat stroke. Karimu sent the driver to find ice and cold drinks, still blaming him for the puncture. Knowing that I didn't have the option of being unwell I drank as much as I could, took Paracetamol and was wrapped in towels soaked in iced water. My body was burning yet I felt so cold.

Dragging myself up, I told the others that I must dress in my new robes. I felt dreadful. They led me carefully to this new celebration, as grand and chaotic as the first. The air pounded with drumming. Dancers from other villages were there to perform for me in between speeches. Village women danced in a wide circle, shuffling round and round. Every so often two broke out of line, faced each other, ran on the spot then leapt to face away from their partner, bumping bottoms. This was a very old, traditional dance, which I had joined in before. This time I managed the shortest of performances, causing huge merriment. The photo of this hit the world press. Even through the music and tumult, another noise was insidiously making room for itself. Dust was beginning to rise as the wind wailed loudly. The air turned dark red, and breathing was difficult. The celebrations were abandoned as everyone took shelter in the homes of the locals. The day was over, except for the trip back to Walewale guesthouse.

Simon had to develop his photos, and had his own satellite system to send them back to his editor in London. Back in Walewale he mystified the fan ladies who, I thought, were part of my enskinment dowry. Later I realised that, if they stuck with me, they would at least be fed. Simon showed them photos of themselves and they were delighted as they had never before seen anything like this. High temperatures interfered with his plans as he needed thirty-five degrees of heat to develop his film. There was no ice and, even at night, that was an unrealistically low temperature. Yet he succeeded and was pleased with his pictures. His work now done, after a close encounter with a bat in his bedroom, he found a car and driver and left. I was sorry to learn that he had picked up an unfortunate infection while with us. Not many escaped from the hazards.

We faced another challenging journey home to U.K. The airline allowed us to take my regalia, four of the very large chief's cushions, as well as my still bloody goatskin. I was even allowed to take my chief's stick. A few years later I realised that I could no longer take this as customs might break it looking for drugs. So it stayed by my kitchen door, becoming more bent with each passing year. No one seemed to notice it, and in Ghana I had another one. Back in Norfolk, I found myself high in the headlines, with a picture on the front page of most newspapers and, of course, SKY TV News.

Visits to Ghana were expensive and caused difficulties and disruption for our team out there. They took great care of me and I always felt welcomed. They were proud of new achievements and honest about obstacles. My trip diary was essential. Reading back, even in 1999, it seemed impossible to me that things wee working so very well.

What follows are tape transcriptions of just a few of my memories of a stay in Walewale in February 1999:

Monday 8th February

Sitting outside, very early in the morning, just watching. Children are already on their way to school. They have nothing so there is no need for a school bag, but some have a pencil slotted through their tightly curled hair. Many don't have shoes, but they greet me as they pass, full of smiles. When they reach school, five miles away for some, they begin their day by sweeping out the classrooms, as goats, sheep and poultry have slept there. They make brooms from sticks. The water cart is making its trip, delivering opaque water for us to wash and cook with. There are many schools now. There seems to be an extra one every year but there are still far from enough places for the huge numbers of children. Some schools are simple shacks, others have no roof, some are collapsing and some have a few desks. All are overcrowded, children packed into classrooms, yet beaming with the joy of being at school.

We've only seen one female teacher in the schools we've visited. This is one of the problems. Girls need role models. Mostly they drop out. We saw Arigu School, and their 'Wulugu' desks are still as good as new. But we have often seen schools and public buildings with broken furniture, that could be repaired, just pushed into a corner. We toured today and saw the results of some of the things we helped with last year. It was particularly good to see the shea butter extraction machinery in Wulugu up and running. The women use it themselves but increase their income by charging women from other villages to crush their shea nuts. They charge the equivalent of two-pence a bowlful. Cost has to be low as the women are so poor. Locals try to bank the money so they have something for times of poor harvest. This is what you'd expect of these extraordinary women. My attendants helped today by protecting me from the punishing sun by making sure I was well covered, and vigorously fanning me while waiting in the heat for a meeting with a chief or other dignitary. There is nothing hierarchical, they are good friends and know that their help is invaluable to their pale-skinned chief.

Tuesday 9th February

Travelling back to Tamale after a meeting with the Vice Chancellor at the new University of Development Studies, scheduled for 11am. This took place surprisingly early for 'Africa time', at noon. I wore my honorary fellowship robes from Sunderland University, as this was an important visit. We had the chance to talk to several students who are very proud of their university and say they are well taught. There are courses in medicine, agriculture and science, as well as development strategy. Hope and optimism are high but they believe that their courses are more difficult than those in the other five Ghanaian Universities. We heard about their loan scheme, and learned students have to do a year's National Service, which means teaching in the North. The government has stopped paying them for their teaching, so they think that the numbers of teachers in the North will drop even further. This is a problem, as National Service teachers play a very important role.

In a senior school in Tamale we gave students letters from English students, asking to set up a linking scheme. We were pleased and surprised that the computer we gave them last year is still working, and in use. The school really needs more books and would like more computers. Next we visited a very large secondary school that is a specialised science centre. The idea was to provide equipment to a number of key schools and have children bussed in from the remoter schools. The problems include lack of fuel for the bus, highly inappropriate equipment, dangerous chemicals, no safe storage and neither sinks nor drains. We gave them a set of football kits from Roker in Sunderland. They have a new computer room, with air-conditioning, but no computers. One of the science teachers told me that any chemistry book would be useful as they have none. I remember another teacher begging for a copy of the Periodic Table. I have no idea how they can teach without access to the basics. It made me think that perhaps we were too selective when sending books, trying not to send anything that's not in best condition, but perhaps we should have sent them all. The headmaster talked about his problems recruiting girls. Sometimes the fathers would rather spend the money buying another wife than paying to educate his daughters.

Wednesday 10th February

Another cool day. In the morning we visited some of the schools near our house in Walewale. Some are Muslim, a few Catholic, some have traditional beliefs, but they don't discriminate and most schools have pupils from various religions. The Regional Director of Education told us that they had a Department For International Development (U.K) grant but are still so short of teachers that they had to shut down some schools. He told us that we should visit Salinga as it needs help with everything. Only one girl from this region went to university last year. Women teachers won't come because they aren't safe in village houses and can't find accommodation. If we could provide this, we could help solve the problem of the low numbers of girls.

At the end of our official visits today we travelled to visit the Nadin family, firm friends and a source of refuge for so many travellers.

We first met the British Nadin family in 1996. They had heard me on the World Service and contacted me in England. They have brought up their family in a very remote compound called' Mango and Monkey,' (because they have a fierce pet monkey living in their mango tree.) Tony has translated the Bible into Mampruli, the local language. They welcome waifs and strays, us included. Today we were pleased to call on them and take a much-needed breather. But I made an embarrassing mistake and put my precious ice straight into an air warmed-glass. It cracked, of course.

Now back at Walewale, early evening but already dark, sitting on the veranda, receiving a constant stream of visitors. Children love to come to chat, a fine way to practise their English. Most of them speak Mampruli, but there are so many different languages in Ghana. Most adult women do not speak English at all and that makes it difficult, but we usually manage to communicate with expressions, signs, and laughter; often the women laughing at me. But they are very kind, always trying to protect me from the punishing sun and from the masses of children who want to touch my skin or hair.'

Publicity rumbled on during the following years. I learned though that, without the celebrity input, we were always going to find it tough to raise funds. It was always pleasing when the North-East press wrote about our work and this encouraged small but vital help from kind and caring locals.

We were delighted that that Beverley, a young reporter from the Sunderland Echo, travelled with us in 2001. She was brave, inquisitive and took amazing photos. That time we stayed in a new, empty large house in Walewale. We had been trying to raise funds to build a vocational school for girls but without success. The locals had begged for help and presented strong arguments that the current generation of older girls were particularly disadvantaged as they had never had any education. Sitting in the porch one evening someone suggested that this house was big enough to begin our vocational school. So that is what we did. It was not ideal, but at lest gave us a start, and cost much less than a proper school.

Eventually, Walewale Vocational School grew from forty to fifteen hundred students. But not without turmoil along the way. Having a bumpy tide for the first few years became the norm for each of our seven vocational schools. This kind of work had rarely, if ever, been done before so there was nothing to learn from. Paradoxically, by 2018, we were one of the major providers of Vocational Training in Ghana and our expertise was in demand.

But there **was always** a lot to learn. Each trip to Ghana was filled with difficulties, triumphs and disappointments but we developed the confidence to be certain that we could overcome the obstacles, however daunting they appeared at the time. I continued to keep careful diaries as our trips were so full-on and so uncomfortable that important things fell out of my head if I didn't write them down almost as they happened.

Beverley was splendid company, and very brave. We used the excuse of Beverley's Birthday more than once to have a very welcome glass of alcohol. (Although everyone was tolerant of our many peculiarities, we were careful not to cause any offence in this largely Muslim society.)

I loved the connection with my home and knowing that friends in Sunderland would be delighted to read her reports in the Sunderland Echo.

We had two very special football kits to give to schools. There was a red and white Sunderland Kit and a black and white Newcastle Kit. Karimu wanted us to take them to a distant small town called Salaga but was unusually cagey when we tried to find out why. So we hit the road yet again, taking overnight bags as the journey would be long although we had not been warned how uncomfortable. This was a different sort of non-road, with tight, high, transverse ridges along its length that shook the truck so much I thought it would fall apart. It also shook the passengers for three long, hot hours. Seat-belts were impossible, cutting into us. But without them heads kept hitting the roof.

I learned that, historically, Salaga was another place known for its connections with slavery. It was a mid-country collection point with regular slave markets. Those captured by the traders must have been completely terrified and many did not survive the next part of the journey down to the coast. But I hadn't learned about the high state of unrest, as war between the Konkombas and Dagombas was thought to be imminent. That explained the road blocks and military presence. However, as we reached our destination, Karimu's plan began to unfold. He had told the locals that we were coming to Salaga to present new football strips to the Konkomba and Dagomba teams, and we would watch the match. That announcement was, remarkably, enough to de-fuse the threatening situation. So war was averted this time. The game resulted in a one all draw.

At the same time, by coincidence, in the North-East of England, a real local derby was being played at Sunderland. Two days later when we landed in Schipol on our return to the UK I saw a group of Sunderland fans in their team shirts and asked them what the result had been.

'Why man, it was a draw, one all, but we were the best.'

So Beverley made the most of this scoop, but The most important thing was that peace returned to Salaga, and we were told that it was all down to our football match!

Chapter 12
Queen of all Philanthropists: The Gonja

One very hot day in June 2003, we drove the rough road as far as the Black Volta. We were going to visit Daboya and see the schools we had helped there. Men and women queued and bantered as they waited for a canoe to carry them to the other side, their children playing in the dust. Eventually, a boat was found that was thought suitable for the 'reverend father.' That's what they called me, as their only other meeting with a white person had been a male missionary.

They loaded us into the canoe. 'Are we safe?' I asked.

'Oh yes, not many boats sink and we will spot the crocodiles,' I was assured.

The crossing was breath taking: such beauty, calm and unspoiled scenery. How privileged I felt to be here in this remote place, being cared for by people who themselves were unspoiled by the greed and wants of today's world. The water lapped gently, another boat from the far side made its way slowly across, the passengers waving their greetings. This was a picture to hold forever in my mind, one that made the difficult times worthwhile. I was to cross here many more times, meeting tribal hostility, facing the kind of dangers that 'ordinary' people don't usually encounter. Funny, I'd always thought of myself as ordinary. As we reached the far side at Daboya, a group of drummers was waiting for me. 'They have come to take us to the durbar,' said Karimu. My heart sank. We had already travelled for hours today and needed to visit three remote schools that we had built as well as meet a number of local officials. A durbar would take half a day and there was no time. We must leave by three pm if we were to have any chance of returning to Tamale by nightfall. Roads at night were too dangerous. It was also essential to visit the Vocational School for Girls at Daboya, a dilapidated and barely resourced school helping girls to sew and cook, so that they could earn a living instead of early marriage and yearly babies. A missionary had established the school but, since he died of some undiagnosed disease, it had been heading for closure. The locals had heard about the vocational school in Walewale that we'd set up, and needed help.

I asked for a toilet, which brought the normal flurry of activity and consternation. I was taken into a house and shown into a room. 'You can use this' they said. But this was a clean room with a pristine floor, and no toilet. Apparently, I was to urinate on the floor and someone would be sent to clean it later. I didn't have the energy to argue, nor could I wait any longer.

We were led up a hill, passing stalls selling all kinds of food. Much of this was tinned, sent no doubt as aid from donors. Every stall had the same piles of tinned pilchards, evaporated milk and beans. There were bottles of cola and lemonade as well as local beer and malted drink. Some had maize meal bread in polythene bags which was yellow and sweet, sometimes tasting of kerosene. Often there were insect egg cases and other insect parts baked in with the loaf. Jam could be bought in some of the newer garage shops near the city, which made the bread edible. We couldn't rely on the local dishes, as risk of intestinal infection and parasites was very high, particularly for non-locals.

The music and drumming grew louder. People were thronging everywhere. 'Come this way.' I was led to a seat protected by shade, amongst the village leaders and dignitaries. They handed the guests a crudely typed sheet headed *Itinerary*. It looked very long and would take hours. I tried to cool myself by using it as a fan.

'Lynne, what is "enskinment"?' asked Anna, the young BBC journalist who was with us on this trip.

'It's when someone is made a chief.'

'Who is being made chief today?' She had read the programme. I had not.

'I'll ask.'

The answer came as a bombshell. 'You, of course.'

'No. No one asked me. Cancel it,' I was frantic.

Anna was jumping around with excitement with her TV camera. This would be such a scoop, would make her career. 'You must!' she shouted above the noise. 'You can't refuse.'

'Watch me.'

'Please, please. It would be amazing to film'

'Did you know about this?' I asked Karimu. 'Surely no one can be chief of two tribes.'

'Yes they can,' he replied. My heart sank.

When I'd first visited Damongo, the main town in Gonjaland, I had been invited to the Paramount Chief's palace. That large, round mud hut had been dark and stiflingly hot. I'd left my shoes outside and bowed my way inside, sitting on the wooden bench that one of the Chief's attendants pointed to. As my eyes became accustomed to the dark I remember a small, wrinkled man sitting on leather cushions and animal skins, holding a staff in one hand, and closely surrounded by his courtiers. The linguist spoke in Gonja on his behalf. This was translated for me. At first the conversation was formal, one of greetings and then thanks for my help in local schools. The large metal teapot was passed around. This time I knew what was coming and everyone keenly accepted one of the narcotic cola nuts from inside. I had known that this was a high infection risk, apart from the drug content of the nut, and, as I had learned in the Mamprugu Paramount Chief's palace, did my best to pretend. The Chief and his minions roared with laughter, and the atmosphere relaxed, laying the foundations for friendship. This Gonja Paramount Chief died four years later. Following my visit, he had left clear instructions to his followers that the next time I came to Gonjaland, I should be enskinned as a Gonja Chief. I'd had no idea!

My Gonja enskinnment was to be carried out by the new Gonja King Wusipewura Yakora Gbedese 2nd, who had arrived on horseback, a sign of prestige, and riding without a saddle. At the ceremony he explained that his predecessor had vowed to enskin me, and today he was fulfilling that promise. This chief had a remarkable history in the army and had served in Japan, Germany and India in the Second World War.

During the ceremony, while the crowds danced to the drums, the curious and brave came to look at the new Chief, to greet me and wish me well. When I danced, village women helped to shield me from the blistering sun, wrapping more cloths around me. The ceremony was captured on film by Anna.

My new title was Kacheto-Wurche, shortened to Ewurche, meaning *Queen of all Philanthropists,* one whose help is unlimited. Another tall order!

The ceremony was overshadowed by the lateness of the day. It would be dark soon. There was no place for visitors to stay here. To get back to base meant a return river crossing then a treacherous road journey made even less safe by the heavy rain that made deep holes and shallow puddles indistinguishable. An hour later, having negotiated for most of the planned dancing and drumming to be put off for another time, I was seated in the middle of the celebration ground, being dressed in my new chief's robes. Each part of the costume was ceremonially put on and taken off three times. I was, as always, too hot. So now, as well as Mamprusi *Chief of Education and Enlightenment* I was *Queen of all Philanthropists* of the Gonja tribe.

On the journey to the hotel, I was too tired to think. I just wanted to be clean and less hot. But when we arrived I was told that several local dignitaries had arrived to meet me. Once more I had to find some spare energy to be able to give them the welcome they deserved after travelling, although my journey had been the longest and most difficult. My feet were certainly the dirtiest. In the welcome cold bath, much later, it took many changes of water to begin to make a difference to the red soil colour of my skin.

Next morning, 6 am, as darkness lifted, the village noises fell into a gentle rhythm. As I sat on the low wall surrounding the veranda, I could hear quiet conversations between those walking by to fetch water and share greetings. Numerous colourful birds sang, as if competing for attention. Guinea fowl families shuffled busily by, gobbling like young turkeys. Goats strolled across the dry earth finding food, and in the cool of the morning the toilet trench surrounding the house didn't smell so much. In the distance the water donkey was pulling its load to one of the houses. This water was opaque, always coming with insects and excreta. It worked well as fertiliser and, if left to settle, was fine for washing.

Later that morning, Mark the proud pig keeper, who Roger had helped a little, came to tell us that something had killed six of his precious stock. He had built the piggery himself and kept it cleaner than some of the places that I stayed in, yet it was hard to see how his precious enterprise could survive. In the end he had to give up. Then Esther, whose father died a couple of years ago, visited with a letter for her English pen friend. She was doing remarkably well, due to the very small financial help from her friend, making it possible for her to go back to school. She hoped to become a nurse. Some years later we learned that she had achieved this, no mean feat for a fatherless child. Behind the guesthouse was one of the schools we had provided desks for. Children arrived early, cheerfully brushing the classroom floors with brooms and shooing out the sheep or cows that had spent the night there.

During the following years there was constant tribal unrest. Our solution to the problem in Salaga was only a temporary and tiny sticking plaster and the more we learned , the more we understood the difficulties.

Karimu wrote: *'In April 2004 there was a very bitter tribal war going on in our part of Ghana. In Northern Ghana there are four major tribes who hold political and traditional powers. These four tribes own the land on which very many other tribes settle and pay allegiance to the Paramount Chiefs of the four tribes. Among these settler tribes is a tribe called the Konkomba. These people are very war-like and primitive. They know no retreat in war. They are mainly farmers. The Konkombas are settled in a very wide area transcending all traditional boundaries. They are all over the area, mixed with other tribes. They are settlers from Togo and they are always on the move, exploiting every fertile land. Sometime last year they wrote to all the four Paramount chiefs demanding their own Paramouncy and traditional area. This meant they wanted to carve lands from the other tribes to create their own. The other tribes naturally could not accept this. As long as the Konkombas are settled on the lands as loyal tenant farmers there is no problem. They don't even pay tribute to the village chief, but their village chiefs have to pay allegiance to the Paramount chiefs. But the Konkombas had been preparing for war for a very long time, knowing that when they put their demands across they would be rejected and they would have to fight. So, in February this year (2004) war broke out. The four tribes had agreed that if one was attacked all should join in. The Mamimbas were attacked first and the Gonjas and Dagombas joined in, but my tribe, the Mamprusi did not join in the war.*

There was so much carnage on a local scale, comparable to what is going on in Rwanda now. For two weeks the government did nothing and there was mass slaughter from all sides. Many schools in the conflict area have been closed. It will take time before life can return to normality in these areas. My people, the Mamprusi, actually betrayed their brothers. The Narumbas, Dagombas and Mamprusi are from common ancestors and their languages are very similar. One would not need to learn the other's language before understanding. So, when the Mamprusi did not attack the Konkombas in their area it was a serious betrayal and we are now so isolated that many of us are embarrassed

.It happens that my tribe is the oldest of the kingdoms and our offshoots include the Mossi Kingdom in present day Burkina Fasso. But we are also now the poorest and most backward in everything. We are living on past glories, which our immediate grandparents did not share in achieving. While the Konkombas were fighting with modern, sophisticated weapons we could only boast of spears and bows and arrows and, at best, single and double-barrel guns. The Konkombas have AK47s and G3s. In no time the Namumbas and Gonjas also acquired better guns, but until now I cannot think of a single modern weapon in Mamprugu. The Konkombas cannot be trusted. I know they will attack one day and yet my people are helpless. It looks like they are carrying the whole world's poverty on their shoulders. It is such a pity. I have tried to talk to a number of chiefs and individuals whom I think can afford to buy guns but nobody seems to take things seriously. Presently we have a very useless Paramount Chief. He never dreamt of ever reaching the throne, but by birth right he was put there and he has been foolish. He is illiterate. At a recent youth meeting there was a standing electric fan. He was mesmerised by this, had never seen one before, and spent the whole meeting watching it. Such *a person has to decide for the whole race in times of tribal conflict. During the months that followed, there was mass slaughter in some villages. Estimates quoted a thousand dead. Medical services were absent. Schools played an important role in sheltering children. So many of the round mud-hut homes were destroyed that 150,000 were displaced.*

▪▪
▪▪

Year by year, I understood more clearly the vast reach of the Gonja people, learning about the depth of conflict with other tribes. Considering their history, they may have been startled that a chief of Mamprugu would invest so much interest in Gonjaland. But I was responsible for working with the people to raise aspiration and hope for the future by ensuring that there were more and better schools. We built the large vocational school for girls at Sawla, not far from the Cote D'Ivoire, where thousands of young women had been sent over the border to work and make money for their families. Mostly they became domestic servants or head porters, carrying goods on their heads from dawn to dusk. They were paid with meagre meals or a place in a yard to sleep. Often they were taken as extra wives, without the status of marriage, many returning home to die. Mole, the largest Game Reserve in Ghana, is in Gonjaland. In the 1940's all villages on the new reserve were relocated, the people being told that they could no longer hunt or forage there. Since this land had supplied all their needs for generations, there was anger and fear. Armed rangers were employed to police the reserve and shoot poachers. The hundreds of families that were moved had to build new mud compounds. There were too few schools and teachers would not willingly come here where life was still lived as it had been by their ancestors. Without education, poverty would continue. There was poor understanding of nutrition and disease, long periods of drought and hunger, resulting in many unnecessary deaths.

Our work around Mole was aimed at changing this. We built schools and repaired those in collapse. Where possible, we built hostels for women teachers and gave the village women income-generating loans

■■■

. There was so much to do and so little funding. I was relieved when Biddick Comprehensive, the largest

Sunderland school supplied desks for two of my new schools. One of these was at Larabanga, the gateway to Mole, and people here were used to visitors. Too often they developed a reputation for aggression when they were refused the money they asked for. But poverty cuts deep when the poor encounter the very rich. The Mole projects aimed to develop alternative means of making a living, and so decrease the poaching that continued in spite of the rangers. Some of the poachers came from China, looking for elephant and rhino tusks, but most were locals needing food to eat and to sell.

The locals helped where they could and small Ghanaian charities supported us with money, much to my surprise. We felt so proud of their support. Local government officials looked me in the eye and promised to help. Some actually did, but in a small way. We built a Junior High School at Kabampe, and the District Assembly gave wood for desks. This project also had help from a conservation-based charity working mainly in East and South Africa. They were becoming more interested in community development and education, so Wulugu was a good fit.

Tourism at Mole was poorly developed, as the road leading from the main Tamale trunk road was so pot-holed and dangerous. There was little information for visitors, but Rangers took groups to see many of the animals. The first night that I was at Mole, a rogue group of elephants destroyed several of the Rangers' houses. In later years the District Chief Executive in charge of Mole made sure that we were not charged for staying there. Once we stayed at the Cocoa Research Institute at Bole. Wherever I went I took a sheet and pillowcase. At Bole the bed was clean and the electricity worked. I looked in on the cook in the kitchen and saw the mass exodus of crawling and flying things when the fridge door was opened. Pot Noodles, a vital part of my luggage, was invented for times like this. I realised that there was no time for me to be laid low by avoidable infections.

Years came and went. In the UK, funding for our work in Ghana was a constant struggle. But the achievements in the impoverished North brought substantially improved lives for tens of thousands. The costs went far beyond the inputs of donors. The benefits to most were more than could be imagined. Better schools meant better futures, healthier communities, less poverty, smaller families.

During this time the work in Ghana was led by Karimu Nachina. He endured taunts from many family members, with accusations of neglect. People knew about the corruption surrounding charities and it was presumed that anyone lucky enough to be working with white man's charities would have wealth. Karimu knew that his people could not move out of poverty while those in privileged positions creamed away what was meant for the poorest. Others had said this too, while somehow managing to meet the demands of friends and family for easy money. Karimu saw corruption in action. For example, he told us about a well-known charity that bid successfully for funds to help in our vocational schools. Yet the numbers of sewing machines and computers that reached their destination was a fraction of what could have been bought if we had been able to spend the money ourselves.

I began to understand more clearly the vast reach of the Gonja people, learning about the depth of conflict with other tribes. Considering their history, they may have been startled that a chief of Mamprugu would invest so much interest in Gonjaland. But I was responsible for working with the people to raise aspiration and hope for the future by ensuring that there were more and better schools. We built the large vocational school for girls at Sawla, not far from the Cote D'Ivoire, where thousands of young women had been sent over the border to work and make money for their families. Mostly they became domestic servants or head porters, carrying goods on their heads from dawn to dusk. They were paid with meagre meals or a place in a yard to sleep. Often they were taken as extra wives, without the status of marriage, many returning home to die. Mole, the largest Game Reserve in Ghana, is in Gonjaland. In the 1940's all villages on the new reserve were relocated, the people being told that they could no longer hunt or forage there. Since this land had supplied all their needs for generations, there was anger and fear. Armed rangers were employed to police the reserve and shoot poachers. The hundreds of families that were moved had to build new mud compounds. There were too few schools and teachers would not willingly come here where life was still lived as it had been by their ancestors. Without education, poverty would continue. Poor understanding of nutrition and disease, together with long periods of drought and hunger, resulted in too many unnecessary deaths.

■■

Our work around Mole was aimed at changing this. We built schools and repaired those in collapse. Where possible, we built hostels for women teachers and gave the received the funding directly.

Although these things were frustrating, it was only part of the story. Whenever funding was given to us directly, more than 98% was put into use in Ghana as intended. Our running costs were tiny.

We were all disappointed about the bank in Ghana that promised desks for a school that Wulugu built. We even put their name on the school name board to show that they had helped. But the desks were 'lost'. Perhaps they had never existed.

Chapter 13
2004 Tauhidea, Buipe and Savelugu

Nothing had prepared me for the poverty in Tauhidea, one of the hundreds of villages isolated not by distance but by tradition and tribal loyalties. This was a land where the structure of the tribe and the family could never be disturbed, a land where food and water were so precious that what a family had, a family fought to keep. Every boy knew his goats, every woman her guinea fowl. Where there were cattle, the whole community knew who owned each animal, who looked after them, and where they would be sold. Cattle could be used to buy a wife for a son, or a second, third or fourth wife for the head of the household. During drought cattle must be watered. When disease struck, they must be tended. But the witch doctor was often too expensive to be called in when children were sick.

Across the river was the new primary school that should help lead many out of poverty. They were later given a six-room hostel for women teachers, as without this, women who were sent to Tauhidea to teach never stayed for long. Being sent to the North was seen as a punishment. For women it meant living in the Chief's house where they were treated as an extra wife, with existing wives letting these strangers know how unwanted they were. They were also emotionally isolated, often hundreds of miles away from their own tribes and families and with no means of communication.

The first school we had built, in 1999, was a small mud construction at Wulugu itself. Villagers worked on the building, which was their pride and joy. The small amount it cost came from a trust fund set up by a true philanthropist. Not a rich woman, but a woman who had missed out on education herself. Maria Schroberer was determined to make up for this by helping girls in need. There was an opening ceremony and her framed photograph was hung in pride of place. This school lasted for over five years, a long time for a basic mud structure. By then as many girls as boys attended regularly. A new school was built in a different part of the village because, apparently, the first one had been 'in the wrong place.' Clearly the then head had displeased some of the villagers and we had not been made aware of the minor but active tribal disputes that were important at the time. I later understood the strength of tribal loyalties, and learned to work with them.

To the outside world, a vocational school head teacher who would only employ staff from her tribe, only allowing girls of her tribe to enrol seemed wrong. But this school functioned well, improving lives for thousands. Girls were brought back from slavery in Cote D'Ivoire. They learned to read and write, secure in the knowledge that a better life awaited them. They learned skills that could be used locally to earn money. Tailoring was the most popular. Historically, as in UK, the men were usually the tailors, but these girls learned to design and to cut patterns. Some became skilled at tie-dye and the technique of batik, producing cloths that were much in demand. Others learned to weave, making the highly prized cloths that men wore as dancing smocks. They learned to count, to measure and calculate. Catering was also popular with a great demand for well cooked food, both at the roadside and in the small catering establishments that were springing up to serve lorry drivers and travellers. While they trained, they ran a school 'chop' bar (a kind of fast-food café) by the road. Selling what they made provided funds for more materials. Teachers needed gas for stoves, as previously all cooking had been done in enormous pots on charcoal outdoor fires. They needed cutlery and crockery so that their students could be employed in small hotels, the Cocoa Research Institute, or hospitals. They could also cater for weddings, funerals and official events. This was all very new; few of the students had ever seen a knife and fork before, or used a saucepan, tablecloth, plate or a serving dish. When I visited they laid on a feast of food they thought I would like; cake, trifle, sausages, but all without refrigeration. The students were proud, talking quickly in good English, even though most of their mothers had never been to school and spoke only Gonja. But the girls had learned to read and write, to weigh and measure, and to calculate costs.

The students at Sawla wrote, rehearsed then performed a play for our visit about the value of education for girls. It was both funny and passionate, yet heart-breaking, showing the need for more schools like theirs. To the girls, it seemed impossible that we had to struggle for the funding for such work. They saw so many charities wasting money, and those who should know better shamelessly diverting money intended for education, telling them that there was none to pay the teachers. They saw that the Wulugu Project did not have large vehicles, grand offices or even any employees. Unlike other charities it was run by their own people voluntarily, although white people helped with funding. The Ghanaian people knew that we were far from wealthy. It was inconceivable to them that no one, and particularly not me, had been paid for the work we were involved in.

While catering and tailoring were the most popular, all girls had classes in entrepreneurship showing them how to set up in their own business or to find more training or a worthwhile job. The trainee hairdressers loved their lessons. They delighted in practising on each other and on the village women who paid a few cedi to have their hair styled. Their tutor bought in some hair products, including the large hair rollers that were in demand to straighten hair. The students needed to learn wig making, as straight hair wigs were popular amongst those who wanted to look less African. When they graduated, they set up businesses in small booths decorated with posters. Since they were from villages across the North of Ghana, there was seldom any competition. Life was good for these girls.

Some wanted secretarial courses. An obstacle for them was the government requirement that they learn using typewriters, as keyboards - no one had any idea why - were not allowed. There were very few typewriters available anywhere in Ghana or even further afield, but the tutors did their best. Although this school was connected to the electricity grid, it was unreliable, only having occasional power, and when the school paid the bill. They needed computers and printers. Some were found from time to time, and the numbers graduating with qualifications in IT were amazing. I received long lists, showing the backgrounds of the students and where they found themselves once their training was completed. Miraculous, considering the hunger, dust, rain, lack of machines, inks, and paper!

Mariam the head teacher here, was a canny woman. She was traditionally built; short and stocky with a constant beaming smile. She planned carefully, and pestered for help like a terrier, storing food for her girls, as many were so poor. She managed to find the help to build two more hostels, housing well over their limit of one hundred and twenty girls each. Girls arrived every week after long bus journeys, and with everything they could carry. They were far from home and family yet settled in quickly, learning the rules, understanding they must keep everything clean. There were 'bathrooms' in the corners of each hostel, where water was brought in buckets. As the girls washed, the wastewater flowed through a hole in the side of the bathroom onto the land outside. When these bathrooms were also used as toilets the stench was unbearable. The actual toilets - long drop - with no water and flat bench seats - were in a separate block. There was no toilet paper, teachers using old test papers or layers from cardboard boxes. Neither were there sanitary towels, the girls making do. But at least here they were not ostracised while menstruating.

Some were married and some were mothers. Many had been sent to vocational school by husbands who saw it as a route to increased prosperity for themselves. Sometimes this arrangement was short-lived as the men realised they could not bring their wives home during the day if they needed them to help with crops or to carry goods to market. Babies simply fitted in, sitting on the tables in the middle of the sewing machines or sleeping on the floor. They were content, not seeming to need the constant attention of babies in England.

Walewale, one of our earliest vocational schools had a particular problem with young mothers. A deep insult was 'born one' meaning that a girl had had only one child, therefore lacking fertility. These girls were mocked in their villages until they became pregnant again. But the students at the vocational schools wanted to complete their courses and to pass examinations that would qualify them for skilled work. It was largely down to the *born one* stigma that the first of the Wulugu Project vocational schools faltered a little after such a promising start. Yet fifteen years later Walewale Vocational School had almost two thousand students. The local education service had adopted the school. In taking on a school that had been improved thanks to Local Government and the Parent Teacher Association, it was fulfilling the directive that every district must have vocational schooling. Nevertheless, the head, after travelling two hundred and fifty difficult miles more than once, was expected to negotiate, meet strict criteria and, in the end, compensate an official in the capital for his time. The school was re-branded: 'Walewale Technical and Vocational Educational Institute' yet, for a time, the curriculum became more academic and less practical, resulting in a complete change in approach to learning. The teachers employed were properly qualified in traditional teaching fields and were to prepare students for academic examinations. There was no room for the trainers of weavers or caterers. These highly skilled people had worked for little pay, passing on their craft to willing students. Now practical work would be rare, with even poorer equipment than before. Although paper is precious, it is much less expensive, of course, than dyes, sewing machines and saucepans.

As often happened, this was overcome and the school flourished as the demand for University decreased when families realised that the degrees often lead no-where.

Boys in Northern Ghana had had access to schools for more than a generation, and if they hadn't taken advantage of this, it was seen as the fault of themselves or their family. But the families were still reaping the legacy of colonisation when education here was the lowest priority. Although pupils are remarkably well-behaved, boys sometimes questioned the need for school discipline. Not for them mornings in packed dusty rooms with a teacher writing notes on a faded board for them to copy. Yet it was amazing that so many learned so much, and I was pleased to be welcomed into many classrooms where we'd provided desks. It was impressive that a youngster of fourteen could tackle differential calculus in the back of a dark and dusty over-crowded classroom. For those boys who dropped out the future only held poverty, and some turned to poaching or joined rebel groups. So the obvious step had been to open up some of our the vocational schools to them too, teaching them block making, painting and electronics.

Three of the most successful vocational schools were taken over by the Local Education Service, but others had difficulties. Daboya had a small tailoring school established by a Catholic priest. When he died, people turned to the Wulugu Project, pleading for help to keep the school open. After tough negotiations and successful fund-raising we were able to build a proper building with a hostel for girls. Shortly afterwards, the government gave Daboya a new status in making it a recognised District. Karimu Nachina was jubilant; sure that this would bring more help. But, for a while, there was little information about the Daboya Vocational School. The river was always too flooded to cross and there were dangerous tribal uprisings. Despite this, a couple of the teachers took part in training days organised for them and colleagues from the other schools. Although they were enthusiastic, they said little about Daboya. Then the truth emerged. This new district had an appointed District Assembly to look after it, and members of the assembly received payment from the government. They did not have an assembly hall or any official offices so they took over the best existing building, which was most of the vocational school.

For a time, the real work of the school took place in makeshift rooms, and teachers did not want to be there. Following a series of gruelling meetings, local government moved out, leaving behind a great deal of damage. They promised to put this right, but did not. Then when they did move out, the new Senior Secondary School moved in. Locals threatened the lives of our team as they saw them, wrongly, as part of a rival tribe, and no-one felt safe.

Things settled again for a time. Undaunted, the team in Ghana restored the school and student numbers increased again, despite difficulties in finding the funding needed to pay the trainers and for replacement equipment.

Despite all the hurdles and disappointments, our vocational School played a life-saving role for the district, with thousands of girls gaining skills and qualifications, many moving on to further education or setting up their own small businesses. Teachers and students from both schools began to share lessons and equipment, with Wulugu keeping a proud and watchful eye.

Savelugu had also been an 'interesting' district at times, and it seemed unwise to establish a vocational school there but it was what the people thought was needed to help defeat the massive poverty. As always, things began well, with a promise of the extension of electricity as far as the school. I felt that this school was too far from the centre of Savelugu, making it difficult for students and teachers to get there. Some of the first equipment was lost, and the housemother living in the girls' hostel, where the numbers of girls were falling, took the key and went away! No-one thought to find a locksmith and cockroaches took over. They also needed a water tank, but as soon as it arrived the tap was stolen before it was connected. Karimu had the tank re-sited in the school compound. Eventually, the promised electricity arrived. The head was surprised to learn that they had to pay the bills and argued her case for help eloquently with the local administration, who blamed the government for giving them insufficient money. Receiving barren promises from the District Chief Executives and their teams in every district we worked with, I decided that such meetings were a complete waste of time. It was better to leave negotiations to our local volunteer teams on the ground. Since they were not employed by the Wulugu Project they were in a strong negotiating position. Their deep understanding of local cultural issues and nuance was invaluable. UK Rotary helped, sending out sewing machines and Trade Aid tailoring boxes containing many useful materials for budding tailoresses. One year these were shared by students in the school, and another year were presented to graduates to use when they set up their own businesses. On one occasion a local Rotary Club from Tamale was involved in presenting the kits.

Savelugu Vocational School clawed its way out of difficulties. One of its greatest strengths was the tailoring teacher, Mary. After school each day she went to teach village women tailoring skills so that they could develop their own small businesses. At the same time, she funded herself through a distance learning teaching course. A remarkable woman.

Local Imams constantly reminded their followers of the importance of sending all girls to school, thus giving the same message as the few stray Reverend Fathers, relics of the Christian missions. Christian churches had followers in the towns, offering long services in ornate, substantially built churches while their converts continued in their poor mud huts. Christians and Muslims lived in harmony with those of no faith. Pork was becoming popular with non-Muslims and the new enterprise of pig farming was becoming problematic. If the pig strayed into the path of a Muslim it might be killed, bringing devastation to pig farmers. We tried to help a young American Peace Corps volunteer working at Wulugu Secondary who wanted to set up a pig and rabbit farm in a school to boost income. The pig venture was very short lived, no-one admitting killing the pigs. The experimental garden in the same school however worked very well. Agriculture students tried growing different crops as food sources with great success. More work was needed to encourage villagers to change their diet, despite the endemic malnutrition that caused so much suffering.

Chapter 14

Tell Her It's Mine Chief

Walking through Tauhidea, on an official visit, I heard a heated argument between two young women teachers behind me. I stopped, took a drink from my water bottle, and asked them if there was a problem. 'It's mine Chief, tell her it's mine,' shouted Maria, the young teacher who, like her companion Comfort, lived in the teachers' hostel. 'I have two sons and a daughter, tell Comfort that I need your empty bottle more than she does.' Recognising that it was my water bottle that was causing the argument, I realised again the depth of poverty and the degrading measures people took to make life more bearable. This problem was easy to solve, there were more bottles of water in the truck. But most difficulties here would be out of my sight and beyond my experience. I was privileged and protected, and pompously thought I had adapted to deprivation, easy for a short time. I understood the value of an empty plastic bottle, and had cut one in half to use myself to transfer water from the donkey-delivered water barrel to wash my hair or take a shower. I had stood outside of Walewale guesthouse with a bucket and half a plastic bottle many times in the blackness of the night, cooling down and washing. There were always spectators, children appearing from no-where to watch the spectacle.

Later during the evenings and in the half light of early mornings visitors would call to sit on the piece of concrete they called a 'veranda', to peacefully and quietly talk about their families, their lives and hopes for the future. Each time we stayed in Walewale they would return with simple delight at being welcomed and remembered. On the surface their lives were so different from those of the white people. In reality, and in so many ways they were just the same. What really mattered was their family. They openly talked about their concerns, worries and hopes and wanted to know about ours. Pressures were increasing as society progressed. Yes, things were hard for the previous generation, but everyone knew their place and these low expectations limited stress. The Chiefs made the rules. Villagers obeyed them.

This was the first generation where girls went to school. The mothers of Tauhidea tried hard to send all their children to school regularly, and this meant managing without the help of their daughters, whereas traditionally, girls were kept at home to help with the chores of the mud compound, carrying water, tending to younger siblings. Without shoes and with only a thin cloth to protect them from the punishing sun, girls carried water long distances so carefully that none was lost. They took clothing to the pond or stream to wash, thrashing them on the rocks and laying them out to dry. They foraged for food in the open land, pounded yams and stirred soup in vast cooking pots on charcoal fires. Sometimes they would walk to market, carrying Shea butter soap or bags of groundnuts to sell. Market days were rotated, each village in the district had a different market day each week.

The ramshackle stalls displayed the frugal goods for sale. There were neat piles of yams, cashew nuts, charcoal and rice. Swarms of flies guarded the shining dried fish. Bush meat was in demand at a high price alongside guinea fowl eggs. The market had a smell of its own. Thin chickens were tied together on a long line of string, no energy to move as the sun beat down on them. Goats and sheep had shade, as they fetched much more if they were alive when sold. Walking between the stalls, traders carried snacks on their heads, including pastry parcels with beans, bananas or coconut inside. Sometimes these snacks were in a protective cage to ward off the flies, sometimes not. Sickness and diarrhoea were a major cause of premature death. Where there had been no schooling, learning about health was passed through generations. Some common cures were more dangerous than the illness.

In the larger village markets were different stalls. Coffin makers did a brisk trade. A shiny coffin was a must, however poor the deceased and their family. For Christian funerals they had to be even more ornate. Funerals were a social highlight for the poor, as there was always food. Children looked forward to a game where they stole the body (sometimes that of a grandparent) and hid it away, not giving it up it until they were paid. All part of the celebrations. Home brewed liquor flowed freely. Drumming and dancing made the air throb. Those travelling from neighbouring villages expected to be found a place to sleep that night.

Other stalls sold locally made cloths and intricately woven local dancing smocks for the men. The smocks cost a great deal to produce, taking weeks to weave and sew.

Increasingly there were new stalls, in competition with the traditional traders. *'The White Man has Died'* stalls had worn garments from Europe, mainly the UK. Wearing a shirt or pair of Western shoes was a symbol of status, as young men would shun local, traditional garments, wanting jeans and socks instead. Older women searched for underwear, some found yellowing overstretched bras long since discarded in Bournemouth or Bridlington. Sometimes the local witch doctor would sit quietly waiting for business. He could cure everything, from AIDS to alcoholism. Further south, and often by the roadside, wooden stalls with roofs formed the more permanent shops. Some of these had tins of sardines, corned beef, biscuits, cheese slices and evaporated milk for sale alongside local produce. The Western items were costly, and many had profited from them before they even reached the stall where they were bought as luxuries, or by foreigners seeking anything resembling food at home. Young white volunteers, too young to be there, were commonly traumatised at first by the deprivation. Whatever they'd been told, nothing prepared them for these food problems, or the stomach infections, lack of water, parasites and heat. Untimely and sudden death was a part of life. Mothers would say: 'She just died, she was sick'. Malaria and malnutrition were common causes, as were measles, meningitis, polio and rabies. HIV/AIDS was not diagnosable by traditional healers, and no one really knew how many died. But some men thought that having sex with babies and young children would protect them from HIV

Children were smaller than those in UK. Most had swollen bellies caused by lack of protein. Their mothers had never been taught about nutrition, and protein was expensive. Those who survived grew tall and strong, their life style forming muscles and calloused hands. Their faces and bodies were scarred by tribal markings, carried out by village elders soon after birth.

Despite the great powers of the Chief, the mystical talents of the sooth-sayer were on a different level. He was revered and sometimes feared. One sweltering evening I was brought to meet one. This wrinkled and gnarled elderly man was sitting quietly, his thin legs crossed on the bare floor in his dark mud hut. Behind him, caged off, the floor was covered with well-worn stones that were free from the red dust that covered every part of the mud dwellings. Formal greetings were exchanged; a long, slow business.

He took a forked stick and began to stir a large group of stones, chanting and gazing ahead into nothing. Suddenly his body jerked, his arms and legs twitched and he began to shake. 'Twins,' he said in his firm Mampruli voice. Then he calmed down, looked up at his guests and invited each to take a handful of stones. One by one he examined the chosen stones, quietly and thoughtfully. He told his visitors that their work here was of more value than he could explain. Each was given a specific task, something small, aiming to help the poorest in the communities. I was told to be at the crossroads at dawn with a fowl and give it to the first hungry person I met. Karimu was instructed to take eggs to a woman whose husband had recently died. The sooth-sayer made no demand for money. He clearly lived a simple life, trying in his own way to make things fairer. All he had in his home was a foam mattress rolled up against the wall, and a wooden bar for a wardrobe, carrying a change of clothes. The window was a gap in the mud bricks with a piece of cloth as a cover. Seats for important visitors had been loaned by the Assemblyman.

The Assemblyman was chosen by the villagers to represent them at the District Assembly. He was selected carefully because he was the only voice of ordinary people that might ever be heard. This Assemblyman was kindly and caring, with tender eyes, who seemed out of place, but not uncomfortable, in his official role. Unlike the politicians, he was also a farmer tending his cattle. He understood life in Tauhidea. He knew the families and was always invited to important family events. Despite the many births, he was always present at outdooring ceremonies.

Infant mortality was high, each survival a triumph. Those who reached outdooring had many problems ahead. Mothers kept their babies strapped by cloths to their backs and crying was rare. Babies were breast-fed, and if a mother were ill another lactating woman would take over for a while. The babies went everywhere. Whatever the mother did, the baby was there, bouncing up and down as their mother worked on the crops or danced at a durbar, sleeping through ear-shattering noise and constantly changing movements. There were no nappies, so old cloths, leaves, moss, whatever could be found would be used. The importance of good nutrition was not understood, and mothers would simply become thinner until their babies were weaned. Where a mother went to work, perhaps as a secretary or as an assistant in a shop on the outskirts of a town, the baby went along too. Older daughters cared for other siblings who were not yet in school, or where there was no school. Female babies were traditionally promised at birth as wives for older men. These men paid the father well as the girl grew, receiving their wife as soon as she began to menstruate. Many men resented the changes in society, wanting their succession of young wives, so they had no interest in the education of girls or in their being allowed to follow a career. Setting up a small business was acceptable, as long as it was near home and would bring money in for the husband. This, at least, was a step forward and helped older girls realise that they did have some control over their lives.

During this stay in the North, Karimu brought some information from one of the thousands of girls whose lives we were helping to improve. It is unusually eloquent but we were assured that it was a genuine attempt to let us know how we had helped.

'My name is Comfort. I think I am about twenty-three years old. My mother is my father's third wife. I have nine brothers and sisters with the same mother. We are twenty-six children in the compound now. Some have passed away.

I did not go to any school, we were too poor. I did not want to be married when I was still a child so my mother thought I should go across the border to be a head porter. She wanted me to have food and could not provide it herself. I was frightened. They spoke a strange language I did not understand. They gave me heavy loads from early morning until after dark. I was so tired. It was not safe. They did not pay me. They gave me food that was not fit to eat and let me sleep outside the house. Then the men came and said I must do as they wanted. I screamed and shouted but they said to be quiet or they would kill me. I hated that life. Then my mother sent a message to say I could come here, to learn to make my own living. I was so happy. Look at that box, that is where I store all my things. I sleep in the hostel with many friends. All the bunks are full, but we lay mats on the floor in between. It is very nice. The mistress is strict. She makes sure we wash and keep everything clean. We take our cloths to the water hole to wash them and bring fresh water back here on our heads. We sing and dance and laugh. Some of my friends had very bad times like mine but they are working hard now and we all feel brave and strong for the future. If we have children, we will send everyone to school, yes all. Our children will never be hungry. We will have money and store up food for times when the crops fail. We will be able to help the whole family.'

A few days later on the long road South having set out at five that morning and we were hot, uncomfortable and I felt unwell. Approaching the outskirts of the city, our driver James' mobile rang. His wife had, on the day he visited the sooth-sayer, delivered healthy twins. Years later I met up with him again, and he told me he'd never understood how the sooth-sayer could have been so certain. It was one of those predictions that had given the man such credibility.

Chapter 15
Dangerous Times

Time spent in Northern Ghana could never be boring. It is a vibrant country with so much colour and life. Of course, there are challenges but somehow adrenalin kicks in and it is not until later that the scale of the dangers faced becomes clear. Travelling by road was always hazardous; the road from Accra to Tamale a death trap. Although this was the major route in Ghana, much of it was a deeply potholed single carriageway. Queues of over-loaded lorries, many leaning dangerously, chugged towards the next city, Kumasi, or further to Tamale or even Burkina Fasso. Like the packed buses, these lorries had extra loads on top, then bags of yams and goats with the arms and legs of passengers hanging over the side. If a lorry tipped over, the road closed until it could be cleared. With no machinery this might take hours. Even worse were the crashes. Mini-bus loads of damaged bodies strewn on the road with large crowds trying to help were a regular, horrific, sight. These buses had painted slogans on the sides, assuring everyone that *God is Good* or *Fortune comes with Patience.*

On one journey, on the main highway, our truck had a tyre blow out. It crossed the road, out of control to face on-coming, speeding traffic. The driver prayed 'Oh God, Oh God,' took his hands off the wheel and crossed himself as we veered across the road. Miraculously we survived.

There was no shelter from the sun, no spare tyre and no means of finding one, so we hitched a ride. Twenty miles on, the scenario was repeated in all its horror. Once was enough, the second unbelievable. In later years there were planes, but plane crashes were frequent. So it was back to the roads, which by then were even more crowded. Flying was cheaper and much faster. It could take two days by road, more if the inevitable breakdown or puncture happened at night or any distance from help. There were days that planes did not operate. Turning up at the airport and being asked to wait was common. Then another wait while a decision was made to find a vehicle and driver in case the same happened the following day. One such day we travelled with a Ghanaian woman, driving through floods that swallowed whole roads. Cooking pots and boxes floated by as the driver frequently began to nod off in the blackness of the night. I was certain that we would be killed and, despite absolute exhaustion, worked hard, mile after mile and hour after hour, to keep her awake. Extreme tiredness and over-heat seem to wreck common sense.

Once our northbound flight hit storms that should have been predicted. The tiny plane was rocked and buffeted and the pilot had no way of knowing where the airport or runway was. It was impossible to see through the lashing rain as lightning flashed constantly through the clouds. Most passengers were crying and praying. After three landing attempts, we heard the announcement – *We are running short of fuel and will return to Accra.* Passengers were hysterical or rigid with fear, gripping their seats and each other. The flight attendants belted themselves to their seats, crossed themselves and prayed. Lights were dimmed and air-conditioning switched off as the fuel ran dangerously low. Yet we landed safely. No one clapped (the normal practice when planes landed) but sat still in shocked silence while the smartly dressed flight attendant made the usual announcement, *We hope you have enjoyed your flight and will travel with us again soon.* No mention that we were back where we had started! Most passengers were Ghanaian. They did not re-attempt the flight, but later the weather eased and, relieved, we flew to Tamale.

At the end of another hectic visit we spent time with the skilled headmaster who was training heads of the six Wulugu Vocational schools that we had opened by then. He was proud of his work and very certain that the participants in his training were gaining in motivation and ability to tackle the many problems. All was running smoothly, and we were having a more restful Saturday before the flight to Accra the next morning. Then, in the middle of the day we were told, 'you must leave now, we are trying to find a car and driver.' My heart sank. The local airport was to shut tomorrow and there were no more flights today. If I was to catch my Sunday night flight from Accra to Amsterdam, travelling by road was the only option. But the rains were causing landslides and closures on the already poor main road South.

A car turned up eventually, with a cracked windscreen and without seat belts. We packed quickly as we needed to get at least half way to Accra in daylight. Driving after dark was too dangerous, particularly for whites, because of bandits. We set off, aiming for Kumasi before nightfall. Once we'd reached this sprawling city it took over an hour to reach the hotel. We needed to find out about the mudslides on the road ahead, and ask about possible detours in order to check in for the Sunday evening flight. But phone connections were down and our driver had disappeared with the car. We knew the road was blocked near NkawNkaw, so we would have to go west, over the hills. We worried that the driver might not return in the morning, but because were so tired we couldn't remember what he looked like. Sunday morning brought breakfast and our driver, who turned up cheerfully, making me feel ashamed that we had doubted him. He smiled, telling us that he would start his drive north again as soon as he dropped us in Accra. These drivers were used to punishing journeys, chewing cola nuts to keep them awake. They knew where fuel could be found and where there might be toilets for white visitors.

There was time to find a snack before checking in at the main airport. We would check in four hours before take-off, then go to one of the big hotels packed with ex-pats, a treat to drink tea after our experiences in the North. After checking in our luggage we stepped outside the door and, before we had time to think (it was very hot and we were exhausted) a taxi pulled up. 'Be fast, close door,' the driver shouted, pulling away with a screech of tyres before we could close the doors. Then we heard a police siren. The car stopped briefly and I fell out onto the road watching the car drive off with Roger and my hand baggage. I thought I might never see my husband again. A few minutes later he was walking back towards me carrying our bags. The rogue driver had panicked and pushed him out. Being prosecuted for operating illegally was one thing, but kidnapping an airport customer was very serious indeed.

I thought back to other lucky escapes, like the night in Walewale that I had opened my door to find a guard with an AK47 standing there, 'Chief, I have been sent to protect you. There is unrest. Chiefs are being beheaded.' Yet again, I decided never to return.

Chapter 16
Ghana - 2007

In the weeks leading up to the next visit to Ghana in 2007, I was concerned about a cough that would not go away. I went to my GP. 'Nothing to worry about,' he said. I should have insisted that he listen to my chest. But if he had the trip would have been called off, and there was so much to do; visiting projects completed since our last visit, checking on progress of all vocational schools, meeting with HIV/AIDs educators as well as local politicians. Then there were the Ghana Education Service officials, religious leaders, chiefs, women's groups, the Department for International Development. On Sunday 17 June we left home early for the flight to Accra via Amsterdam. In Accra, after the normal battle to get out of the airport, we were met by Karimu and taken to the Miklin hotel for a few hours sleep. The city was waking up as we travelled back to the airport next morning. Charcoal fires burned at the roadside and colourfully dressed women, carrying everything from tomatoes to tables on their heads, were striding along the roadside. It was too early for the beggars

187

or hawkers that would later swoop at slowing vehicles at traffic lights or junctions, waving bars of soap, packets of chewing gum and bags of nuts. Some would run alongside cars, others, often with distressing disabilities just sat very near to the moving traffic, holding out their hands.

The flight north to Tamale worked this time. A relief. We would usually have set out from Tamale the same day, but we rested as this hotel was a palace compared with the Walewale Guest House. As we went to the bank to get our cedis the bank manager warned us of the almost daily power cuts. Electricity was generated by the Volta Dam, and the Volta was very low. We were driven to the meeting with the Regional Director of Education to remind him of promises made by his predecessor. These included enabling Tauhidea women to learn to read and write, the provision of books for Walewale Vocational School and the speeding up of the proposed adoption of our vocational schools by Ghana Education Service. Yet, in reality, we knew that this would not happen. I still kept a diary.

Tues 19th June 2007

Dawn broke at six am, as it did every day of the year here because we were so near to the equator. We listened to the morning sounds of Africa, as even in the city the birds sang ceaselessly. It was a very hot day with unseasonable temperatures of over 100 degrees Fahrenheit. There was no electricity. The hotel had a working generator but, despite this, the dining room was an oven with a constantly switched on television showing football matches, with staff turning up the sound as we ordered breakfast. There was omelette and sweet bread with a kind of marmalade and fruit. The road to Walewale no longer took three hours. Road repairs cut this by half. Here we met with the District Chief Executive, Zac, an old friend who'd helped us in the past. Once, when our truck broke down, he let us use his official car. He was a science teacher and the head of a local village school for a while. The assembly buildings were being revamped. On the notice board was a sign informing visitors how to obtain a permit to prospect for gold. There is a lot of gold in Mamprugu, which is still not legally mined, and I was well aware that profits would never reach those who needed help. The new oil field off the coast, intended to lower poverty levels, had made no difference at all to those in the North.

We visited Nassirya Primary, which was almost complete the last time I was there. It was now in full use with good management and a two-year action plan. However, the numbers of girls were still too low so more work was needed here on recruitment. I was tired. Considering just how unwell I actually was, this was hardly surprising. My lungs were struggling. We then travelled to Gbani primary. This has much larger rooms. Again, the number of girls was low as this was the height of the Shea nut season. Shea nuts are used to extract oil and make soap and body creams. Sometimes there were buyers from European and USA cosmetics companies. They paid very little. Whenever I saw products at home boasting about their Shea butter content I thought about the thousands of women working so hard to extract it. Shea nuts grew wild. Although they were planting more, the bushes needed reliable water to establish themselves.

Driving to Wulugu Senior High, brought memories of the start of my work in Ghana. This school, where Karimu was the first head, had done so well. We took linking letters from Dartford Girls' Grammar, followed up on six girls sponsored last year by The Commonwealth Countries League and began to collect information about another six. As always, we enjoyed meeting the fresh-faced young American Peace Corps worker who taught science at the school. We inspected the girls' hostel built by the Wulugu Project and, as always, it was full and successful. There were some problems with drains that the headmaster promised to sort out. In reality, there were no drains, only openings at the base of the' bathroom wall'. A piece of pipe carrying waste further away might have helped. Still extremely hot we drove to Tauhidea to meet women who had waited all day for us to tell us about the success of the loan system we had set up there, but by now it was very late. They apologised and agreed to re-schedule this meeting for first call Saturday so that we would not interfere with the daily Shea nut collection.

Back in Tamale it took several changes of bath water to deal with the in-grained red dust and dirt of the day. For the locals, half a bucket of already-muddy water was all that they could use to wash. Most of them wore clean clothes, which were ironed with charcoal-filled irons. Women liked to have European tee shirts, never mind how old, with traditional cloth wraps around the chest to hold a baby. I chose my own clothes carefully for my visits to Ghana. They needed to be opaque even when wet, they must be large enough to allow airflow; they must be cotton and cover most of my body. So I always wore the same dresses for VIP meetings, and the same skirt and top at other formal occasions. Carrying water took up much of the day for women here and was simply accepted as their role. The only time I ever saw men carrying water was when a severe drought hit Tamale. The nearest water was seven miles away and that source was linked to the cholera outbreak. As usual at such times, there were too many deaths.

20th June

An early start to sort out football kits before a breakfast meeting with the local Wulugu team. Next a ninety minute drive south to Buipe on a good road. This was a new community with no post-primary education. They applied to Wulugu for help some time ago, but as always we checked carefully on the current need, as well as the capacity of the local community to support it. In Buipe there were meetings with leaders of the administration team and the newly appointed Chief Inspector of Police. All expressed gratitude and amazement at the speed and quality of our building work and said that the whole community felt that their prayers had been answered, valuing the chance of education for many girls who had been brought back from kayayo (head portering). To my relief their vocational school and hostel looked marvellous, from the toilets to the water-harvesting system. All sectors of community came to meet us at the durbar ground where opening prayers were said by the chief Imam and his entourage. They were translated into English in whispers. Closing prayers were said by a Christian priest. This cooperation between religions was vital and it just seemed to happen. As usual there were long speeches, gifts, dancing and drumming. Goodness knows where they found the biggest, loudest sound system ever. There was electricity too, so an unpredictable sound system boomed away at all the wrong times. The best part was a drama by the girls to illustrate the importance of education. It was funny, yet serious, an experience that made me feel privileged to be involved. They had brought in a boy to play the chief. His swagger, attitude to others and slow movements mirrored the way chiefs behaved and he made everyone laugh despite the serious message of the performance. Ghana TV turned up eventually, but too late to film. They were upset as this meant they would not be given the hand out they had anticipated. Media people expected to be paid by those they filmed. I solemnly cut the ribbon to officially open the school. During the rapid tour of the school I met well-committed teachers and a professional and organized headmistress. Girls proudly showed off wonderful displays of work, and a catering display including spatchcock chicken and celebration cake.

By the third year of the Buipe project –(another newly designated District) – people realised that the school could not run without students and students would not appear if communities didn't know about the school. The school was frequently shown off to visitors and used as a venue for large meetings or training, but student recruitment had been forgotten

Once staff and local government realised they actually needed to invest time in making things work, the improvement was staggering. PTA and local government, supported by the Chief of Buipe, added many more classrooms and a second hostel. They had flush toilets that actually worked. Ghana Education absorbed the school at the peak of its success, employed many more teachers and a new head. I was delighted to meet two smart, vibrant young women who were employed in finance and administration by the well-educated Chief. They were ex-students of one of our more established vocational schools and particularly wanted to say 'thanks' for our help.

Thursday 21st June

Another six am. start so no breakfast! We called at a primary school that would be twinned with a Sunderland school, and filmed pupils individually greeting pen pals. This took a long time but was well worth the effort. I presented a football kit and ball. This always brought a great cheer. For some reason, giving a school a kit always led to better attendance, but there was sometimes a risk that it might be sold without trace, so we promised to call back to watch a match. The children were having a Cultural Experience lesson. Although educationally deprived, this community was not as traditional as Daboya where they still called me 'Holy Father'. Next we returned to the vocational school at Buipe for workshops with HIV/AIDS prevention teachers who had been trained to work with local schools and villagers in the most remote areas. All the original group of thirty-five turned up, coming from distant villages deep in the bush. With the help of locals, who were running the training I ran a session to review what had been achieved, with each participating teacher receiving a bag from the Charities Foundation, some lunch and a small amount of money for travel. Ideally funding will be found to enablie this model to be replicated in other districts. I spent the blazingly hot afternoon talking to teachers, the head and girls, who had made me yet another beautiful outfit from intricately patterned cloth.

The headmistress wanted many things, as heads always do. Top of her list was accommodation for teachers to guard the girls in the hostel and prevent them from escaping into the town at night. I told her about other schools where the teacher in charge of the girls had a private room built into a corner of the hostel. Some of these girls at Buipe had come from Afram Plains, East of Nkawnkaw, a hundred and fifty miles away. It was a tough call for their families to send them so far away but they were passionate about helping their older girls to have these opportunities beyond early marriage. Girls paid a small fee each term and the money used to replace materials for practical courses.

On the way back we passed through Tamale to Savelugu to see the newly constructed vocational school, where work was progressing well. Again, there seemed to be a great deal of community support and tremendous need to help move girls out of poverty. I regretted that no funding was available for a hostel there. I did not know at the time that a UK trust was closing and would give me the residue to build one. Back in Tamale I arranged to see the UK Department for International Development in Accra. There was still no electricity here in Tamale and I was exhausted. I had swollen feet but did not connect that with my cough. I had a sore throat, probably from the dust and making speeches and talking all day and I an upset stomach all night.

Friday 22nd June

Another difficult journey to Daboya; two hours of rough road then across the White Volta in a Canoe. It was hotter than ever. We walked to the Chief's palace. Drummers came to meet their white Gonja Chief, walking in front and behind me, playing louder and louder as I moved to the Palace. The Daboya chief expressed thanks, particularly for the new hostel for girls that would open in September with a new intake. He was questioned about two fans that had gone missing. He told them that they hoped to have a police station soon to deal with such things, but that they were all outraged by the theft. Following the usual cola nut ritual, the talking drums carried on playing on the long walk to the vocational school. The red sandy soil was so hot that I had to walk carefully. It would burn my feet if I walked off the edge of my sandals. All looked good at this school. They needed more typewriters and sewing machines as well as paper and material. Many of the girls here were married, in school with their babies, really glad of this opportunity. The school wanted certificates to show that they had completed courses, and this was arranged. They could print them themselves and I would sign them.

Sat 23rd June

That night my insides were very upset. I knew that the electricity outage meant that food at the hotel had not been refrigerated. The following day we again travelled the long road to Daboya. We crossed the White Volta by a canoe already low in the water, and I tried to find a reasonably dry place to sit as we crossed, watching the breath-taking beauty of the trees, the many species of brightly coloured birds and the threatening vultures. Once across, we walked up the hill to a meeting with representatives of women's groups from three communities that had been given income-generating loans. The women watched me. To them I was a lifesaver and I greeted each one with a smile and a handshake. The women of Daboya were early recipients of loans. They had used these for a soap-making project. Although this project was not as successful as hoped, the women felt that the loans had meant survival during a very hard period as well as enabling them to send children to the new primary school that we had built.

Langbinsi women came by foot in their most colourful clothes, bright green and red. Here there was no trace of the recycled Western clothes that were beginning to appear everywhere. The price of Shea nuts was currently low. Although they could repay, they requested an extension of their loans until January when they would get a better price for the nuts, having a profit to work with next year. Bowina women had walked sixteen miles down a tractor track in the heat of over a hundred degrees to see the white people. They were the best organised of all and, despite their poor literacy, had full records, signed when loans were given and repaid. Most had repaid, with interest, part or all within seven months. Since I already knew that Shea nuts were not fetching a good price, we agreed that the women were given back the repayments in order to ensure they raise enough to run their businesses for the next two years.

Eventually there was a long, melting walk back to the Volta. I was so very tired, an unusual feeling for me. I wanted to be carried although I could not ask for help without admitting to being unwell. Many hours later we were back in Tamale where I wrote *tomorrow shouldn't be too hard*! I slept badly, felt unwell, coughed all night with an aching chest, a stomach ache and a strange bite on my back, still having no idea just how sick I was. The following day brought another early start to reach Tauhidea to meet women, including the head teacher. They had loans of half a million cedis (£28 approx) and had repaid. Again, they had not raised enough to run properly next year so we decided to help further. Possibly some, if not all, would receive a million cedis. (During these years the value of local currency was so low that we had to use carrier bags to carry it). It seems that the original loan was spread over a larger group than intended so the money had not really been enough. Eventually, all of the loans, wherever they were given, were successful, in that the women were well organised, with intent of repayment, and enabling children to go to school. A small price if each has ten children. The women were happy about this very real difference to their lives. They were reminded that Wulugu Project was still working with the Regional Director to make a literacy programme available for them. I was meeting more and more similar requests, as women did not want to be left behind. The Tauhidea head seemed to run his school well, despite difficulties. One of the major problems, as for all schools, was the unreliability of the supply of pay for teachers. Pay came from the government although it was often months late. But the school was thriving. Next that day was a visit to Walewale Vocational School for a meeting with the new head, a governor and teachers. It seemed clear that management needed to improve, and we made it clear that we expected more and that they needed to do better. Yet as usual, the positives were amazing. A number of girls had gained vocational qualifications and some had even moved into Senior High School. We had steadily helped the school to grow so, by now, the original large house was not really useful. This building needed some renovation. The current head was living there and was told that he must move out, as this would make the sale more likely. Later there were more meetings with prominent people and many promises were made. Back in

Tamale, late afternoon lunch clearly had extra nutrients, encouraged by the lack of refrigeration. This brought another turbulent night before a meeting with the Wulugu Project Ghana accountant, a tall, slim and very earnest young man, Isaac, who brought photocopies for the treasurer in the UK. His day job was at the new VAT department.

Before travelling to Tamale airport there was a meeting with the Ghana coordinator and his team to check on priorities. The District Chief Executive from Walewale phoned to re-assure us that he would pay personal attention to the vocational school. In Accra, the truck the hotel had sent to meet us at the airport didn't turn up. Roger was having major stomach problems so I needed to be alert. The crowds, torrential rain and dust made thinking difficult. When the truck came, the cases were put in the open back. I thought they might be stolen. I was also worried about Roger who was in the front and feeling terrible. The driver had left us to look for someone else he had to collect. It was raining harder now, with people thronging around us. Eventually we reached the small hotel in Accra where we had a meeting with two of my colleagues in science education, John Tufuor and Mary Gyang, to check all HIV materials being prepared for science teachers. These had been designed at a three-day workshop for health leaders and science teachers from Ghana, Gambia, Nigeria and Cameroon. The following day saw another early start to travel to the centre of Accra to meet The Department for International Development. Traffic was heavy. My chest hurt and I could no longer hide my cough. But I managed the meeting. DFID had expressed interest in Vocational Training and promised to fly officials north to see the Walewale and Savelugu Vocational Schools. Of course, they would not get to the remote ones at Daboya and Buipe.

We checked in our baggage at Kotoka airport. The plane was delayed and baggage was lost in Amsterdam, but eventually we arrived home at 10.30 am Tuesday. I was clearly unwell, but glad to have managed the trip. I thought that what had been achieved was astounding and knew that it had been made possible by the faith that donors had in the ability of the Wulugu teams to maximize return for their money, as well as the dedication, integrity and honesty of the workers on the ground, and incredible work by those in the UK.

Two weeks later I almost died.

Chapter 17
Close Encounter

Back in the UK, our G.P.listened to my chest and sent me straight to the hospital for an X-ray. There was a call almost as soon as I arrived home from there, asking me to return quickly to see a doctor who told me that my heart was enlarged and badly damaged. The most likely cause was a virus picked up in Africa on an earlier trip. I was shocked, felt that this was not fair at all, but did not really believe it. Then I met the cardiologist who began to look at drug treatments; the outlook was bleak. But I did skate in the *Around the World on Ice* dance show on the eighth of July at Norwich ice rink Perhaps not the wisest decision but we had rehearsed for weeks. On Friday the thirteenth I picked up Richard, our son in law, from Wymondham rail station. Soon after arriving at the house I fell over. Richard found neither pulse nor breath, yet kept me alive for eight minutes until the paramedics, who had talked him through the process of resuscitation, arrived. They said that I might not survive for long, and that if I did, would be unlikely to be able to do anything for myself again. Three days in intensive care were followed by a long stretch in the cardiac ward. They had cooled my body with ice to lessen any damage to my brain but were doubtful about recovery. The family dropped everything and came to Norfolk. Jill, my little sister read to me in the hope that I might hear. Roger held my hand, and my lovely daughters watched and waited. When I was later told what had happened I had no memory of any of it, but heard that, while I was in hospital, people prayed; Imams in Africa, Catholic nuns in India, local village churches and city cathedrals.

There had been a problem with the rhythm of my heartbeat. It went out of control, stopped beating, and the ambulance team had shocked me back into life. Now I would have my own device implanted in my chest, a small machine that would be my guardian angel and deliver the current I needed should things go wrong again. So I went home, to be cared for by a family who loved me, and to face a regime of increasing medication. Slowly, day-by-day, my heart improved, and I began to believe that life would go on. My heart seemed to have miraculously repaired itself. The leads that fluttered in my heart were metallic, meaning that I could never have an MRI scan, thus making diagnosis of later health problems incomplete.

The medics said that it was too dangerous to remove the device. The heart drugs meant that there were other drugs I must avoid. When I had influenza the crippling pain was poorly controlled, and took a long time to lessen when I recovered. I never considered going back to work or claiming support. I was simply happy to be alive. Luckily we had always lived very simply. Our childhoods had taught us not to need things.

Years passed and I began to forget about the machine in my chest. I learned to cope and knew I was lucky to be alive. My time was filled by running the charity and with newly arriving grandchildren as well as visiting my mother in Sunderland as she grew more frail. There were five grandchildren who, as they grew, learned a little of the Ghana work but couldn't really understand it. I sometimes felt that I didn't either. It was only really while I was in Ghana that the magnitude of what we were achieving became real.

In 2016 the battery sewn into my chest needed to be replaced. It was astonishing that this internal defibrillator had sat quietly for more than nine years doing nothing, as my heart had become strong again. There were two attempts to change the battery. The first was painful and left an ugly, prominent lump. The second revealed a problem with the leads to my heart, possibly caused by the first attempt. This procedure left me with a debilitating chest infection. I decided to participate in the first UK trial to withdraw heart drugs from patients who had recovered from dilated cardiomyopathy. I also decided to close the charity. Then the message came from the new female head of our first vocational school describing its successes with fifteen hundred students, over fifty teachers and a set of four schoolhouses. One of these schoolhouses was named 'Karimu', another 'Lynne.' I changed my mind about shutting the charity down. Again. Wulugu changed lives and there were thousands more who needed it. Of course, I carried on with my work and was certain that this work would continue without me if I did give up. This had been firmly demonstrated during my major break in 2007. No-one is essential!

Chapter 18
Chief of Peace and Friendship, 2012

The new Vocational School for girls at Karaga was open. The community had pleaded with Karimu and his team for help. There was no school at all for older children. The chief gave the land in a place that I thought was too far from the town centre. The argument was that this land was safe from annual flooding. A representative of a major charity, with offices far superior to those of the local government praised Wulugu and pledged to work to support the new school but by now I knew better than to anticipate fruition of promises. The Chief of Karaga hosted us in his palace. He gave me intricately woven cloths and the women wound them around me and he promised that electricity poles would be extended to the school. In one of the long speeches, through his linguist, he announced that he intended to enskin me. While this would have been the third major tribe to give me this honour, the day had been long enough already. Although the journey was just three hours we were drowning in meetings. 'I am truly honoured'

I said, 'but time is not on our side. We will be unsafe travelling back in the dark.'

We left with a goat and a promise that on my next visit I would become Chief of the Dagomba people. On the way back to Tamale we stopped to watch the crocodiles settling down for the night at one of the water holes. Charcoal fires glowed red in the gloom, sometimes shining fleetingly on faces as they passed by. Pot-bellied, smiling children waved with excitement at the white woman in the car. These villages were only fifty miles from the city but might as well be in a different continent. Few would ever travel beyond the neighbouring villages. Their way of life was as it had always been. They did not need furniture or shoes or toys. Neither did they need books, the internet or shops or coffee bars. They did, however, need clean water, doctors and schools. All the children were small for their age. Most had skin disease or worms or both. They were hopeful for the future and thankful for a place to sleep each night. They knew they would have to help with cleaning and carrying, as that's what children did here. Mothers too were cheerful, but they worried about their children, about which one would die next. They often felt helpless when famine returned, as it always did. Their efforts to keep food for these times were always thwarted. Everything spare was needed for the next funeral celebration, or the chief would demand another toll. I could see how much work there was still to do and felt, as I often did, (but only briefly) defeated. The task seemed impossible. Then I remembered the hundreds of villages where lives were massively improved, where we had made it possible for children to be in school to learn not just to read and write but to understand how to avoid the greatest dangers and difficulties of their environment. I was meeting confident young adults greeting me with, 'Chief, you remember me? I'm from Gbimsi.' Gbimsi could have been substituted by well over two hundred more village names.

In 2012 Karaga established a hostel for girls at the vocational school and we returned for the promised enskinnment. Teachers were in place, and I went to look at the school, officially opened the hostel and enjoyed talking informally to students and teachers. There was a large new building right beside the school. 'Yes, that's the Senior High,' I was told, surprised that that no one had mentioned this important development to me earlier. In the catering department of the vocational school there were crowds of students, all in starched white aprons and hats. Our vocational school and the Senior High were sharing teachers and facilities and it seemed to be working well for now. Vocational schools have presented so many difficulties but the eventual outcomes are usually well worth the battles.

The Karaga Chief and his entourage hurried me away to the durbar ground where crowds were gathering. As I took my place on shining goatskin cushions, the music grew louder. Drums throbbed, whistles shrieked and people dressed in their finest cloths danced for me. Then a gnarled elderly man appeared with a primitive bugle in his hand, his cheeks blowing out like small balloons. The bugle shrieked, hurting my ears. Then the small boy standing next to him did the same. His young face was distorted as his cheeks inflated. I thought they might burst. His bugle made an astonishing noise. On and on went the buglers, and then the air suddenly vibrated with gunshot. A group of the chief's men had rifles that looked homemade and primitive but made impressive gunfire. This was to herald the official arrival of the chief who slowly and regally, in a chief-like manner, walked with his entourage to take his throne. Chiefs always walked slowly, with a swagger, and were protected from the sun by a large umbrella carried by an assistant, perhaps the 'spearman' There was more dancing, more drumming and long speeches. Then I was escorted to the Chief who made the announcement. Handmaidens dressed me carefully in cloths woven in green and gold. They danced, cheered, shared cola nuts, and drank the local beer, Pito, dripping sweat onto the mud floor. My official Dagomba title was *Simni Boma Naa Napagna: Chief of Peace and Friendship*: a rather daunting name to live up to.

Meanwhile, plans for the progress of our vocational girls' school gradually took shape, even though the Senior High took over the hostel at one stage, filling it with their own students. While the Senior High was another important step for Karaga, locals seemed to lose interest in the vocational school. Teachers were unpaid, and many left. There was no move to recruit students, although those in charge had promised to do so. I was annoyed rather than surprised, as we had seen this pattern in most of our six existing vocational schools and knew that the school had already trained many girls. But the vocational school needed nurturing. Part of this involved making sure that the teachers came to the series of training sessions for Wulugu vocational teachers. The Ghana management team set about re-gaining the whole Karaga hostel and fixed any small repairs. The vocational school then began to grow, with many illiterate girls who had been in slavery returning and learning a skill that they could use to set up their own small business, or as a paper qualification for employment, or to enrol for Senior High education that could lead to university. The numbers of graduates from our vocational schools who were playing important roles in their own districts was increasing each year. If ever I felt downcast, I looked at Walewale where the initial small intake of girls was moving towards two thousand.

Karimu and I worked with mutual trust and respect. So many worthy cases for help had to be rejected as our funding was small. While I was applauded for our work, Karimu dealt with the numerous requests for help with empathy and wisdom. There were other charities based in Tamale supporting girls' education. They had large air-conditioned offices and trucks, and salaried staff. But Wulugu was clearly meeting the needs of the poorest and reaching the most neglected districts. It was cheering when local charities and local people helped, and this was happening more and more. I was no longer surprised that people in the area sometimes expected payment for their involvement. They had learned that white man's charities were rich. They did recognise fairly quickly that our funding would not stretch to any extra payments. Those we worked with were always firmly warned that we were different, and we always managed.

We should probably not have been surprised in 2004 when we had a problem getting a container full of books and sewing machines from the port to the North. I'd had to waste precious days in Accra organising the release of the container without paying the high costs that customs 'required'. Our car eventually followed the container for a hundred of the almost three hundred mile journey North. Sometimes containers would be ferried along the Volta for part of the journey. It was never straightforward. In the following years we still had many offers of books but, with regret, declined them all. We simply did not have the number of people needed to collect and sort or to battle with port authorities. Those who had helped us to collect books, pack them and deliver them to the port of Felixtowe were surprised that none of the materials they dispatched from the UK were lost on the way. They had been told that one of the reasons for lack of books and equipment in the remote northern schools was that those paid to deliver them simply dumped them in the bush, as the journey was too long. Yet more than ten years after we stopped sending books we came across schools where the only learning materials were those donated by UK schools.

Over the years there were, sometimes, instances of large charities who seemed to disparage and discourage the smaller ones. Perhaps we were naïve as we found that they were pleased to have help where appropriate, but usually would not consider assisting Wulugu. Nevertheless, help from Ghana-based charities gradually increased and was, in many ways, so important as it showed the world that those benefiting from Wulugu saw it as a real partner, not simply a rich donor.

Chapter 19
2014 Karimu Dies

While living in the village of Murugu, supervising the building of a long-needed primary school, Karimu felt unwell. He was short of breath and too tired to walk. It was neither malaria, nor a common stomach disorder. Eventually he told the workers there that he needed help. Five hours driving on a flooded road brought him home to Tamale. Despite limited diagnostic tools the doctors suspected that he had a heart problem. He was desperate to talk to me. Mamprusi Man, Joseph Karimu Nachina, reached for his phone. 'Hello Poanaba, it's me, Karimu.' My heart jumped. Usually, a call to me on holiday meant a major problem. 'I am in hospital Chief.'

I was sure that, if moved to Accra, he would be effectively treated and recover. So, with Solomon his eldest son, he travelled to the main hospital in Accra where they diagnosed a blockage of the coronary arteries. In the UK, this would need an angiogram, and then a stent. In Ghana neither of these were available.

I flew home from my Rhodes holiday, expecting to be able to contact someone in Ghana to deal with it. But I was told that in cases like his patients need to go to India, South Africa or the UK. He was too ill to travel. Talking to Karimu on the phone it was clear that he was becoming increasingly unwell. The doctors said that although his heart wasn't damaged by a heart attack, he needed treatment. His breathing became more troubled and he could not eat. In desperation I called in favours. The first was to find an estimate for the costs to properly diagnose and treat him. I was not asking for money, just advice, yet the lack of interest from those in a position to help was an eye opener. I made insistent calls to influential Ghanaians who had reason to be thankful for Karimu's great work. Response was sometimes sympathetic, but usually dismissive. My argument for intervention was that this man had made dramatic improvements in the lives of tens of thousands of people in twenty years. Given another twenty, this would be repeated.

In Ghana the House of Chiefs is equivalent to, but probably more influential than, the House of Lords in the UK. Yet even the President of the House of Chief's call to Karimu's doctor drew a blank. One warm, dark October evening my phone rang in Norfolk. It was Isaac, our Ghana treasurer. 'Karimu is unconscious,' he said. As the following day went by with no news, I became hopeful that he might be recovering. But that afternoon, Mr Saffo, a dear, wise friend, called saying 'the body is being embalmed. It will be taken to Tamale tomorrow.' I was in shock.

The days that followed were chaotic and confused. In Accra there were formalities and an ambulance to be hired to take Karimu's body on the long journey back to the North. Petty politics abounded, making sure that I had no chance to come to terms with Karimu's death. His body was first placed in the morgue at the University Medical School. The family involved me in funeral preparations, needing me to mourn with them.

Experience and common sense told me that attempting to get to the funeral would be unwise. It would be in Lukula, Karimu's home village, which was over five hours drive on uncertain tracks from Tamale. Even getting to Accra from the UK would be problematic as there were vaccinations to up-date and the visa process was long and unpredictable. It was extremely unlikely that we would arrive on time. Once the family in Ghana accepted that I could not be there, funeral planning began in earnest. . The family travelled south to Kumasi to find a coffin they liked, as locally coffins were made of rough wood, bought at the market or from the coffin-maker. The body was taken back to Tamale, then to his home village of Lukula. Funerals in many African countries are elaborate, long and expensive, the celebrations greater than for weddings or other occasions. Some families in Ghana spent everything they had when the head of the family died, selling cattle and stored food and even daughters to feed the mourners. If someone was very unwell, money would not be used on a doctor or sooth-sayer, but kept for the funeral. Karimu's funeral had to be magnificent. He had transformed the lives of tens of thousands of the very poorest in the North, yet he was not a rich man, living on a small pension from his education work and taking nothing from the charity. Hi family were expected to host all who attended, meaning food and entertainment for thousands. Bags of rice were brought from Tamale. Locals provided floor space for sleeping and desks were piled up to make room on school floors. The burial ground was carefully prepared as tributes reached the family from across the North and beyond.

Grandchildren played the traditional body-snatching game—stealing and hiding the body, demanding a ransom.

The funeral was Christian, although most attending were Muslim or had traditional beliefs. It took two days. The first was spent in mourning and burying the body, for the reading of tributes, and much praying and wailing. The second was for celebration. More tributes were read, including one from The English Chief. I was touched when they called me his 'Partner'. Local beer flowed and praises for Karimu became increasingly elaborate. They told us that this was a funeral that wouldn't be forgotten. I was so sorry to have missed it but we continued our strong support for this vibrant Lukula village, where education was thriving, by building another much-needed post primary school.

Chapter 20

Karimu's Legacy

I, his Poanaba, grieved. Yet the belief in Ghana that the spirit lives on was so deep that we were all certain that his work would continue. Solomon had played an increasingly important role as his father's work developed, and was in a strong position to take this on, but only with full approval and support of others. Eventually, official meetings with rounds of voting brought Solomon to the helm. Karimu's work went from strength to strength in the hands of his son. With astounding efficiency and wisdom, the key players in Northern Ghana came together, determined to build on Karimu's legacy. The Management Board was re-structured, and volunteers felt free to express their opinions, meaning that Karimu's very traditional approach would gradually and inevitably change. This was the beginning of a new era, one where the past needed to be recognised, celebrated and built on but not allowed to hold up progress. The way ahead was a maze of possibilities and problems. I thought carefully about my own part in all this.

My traditional role was still significant and our work was far from finished. My role now was to be gently but firmly in charge until Karimu's successors were confident enough to plan realistically, and deal with the pressures from others to choose their village, their school or their women's group for support. In the weeks following the funeral, funding for a second school on the edge of the Mole Game Reserve made Murugu Primary a reality. A hostel for teachers was built at neighbouring Larabanga, and by 2016 there were seven vocational schools.

In June that year, it seemed that the whole of Northern Ghana had been involved in planning a grand durbar to celebrate the life of Karimu Nachina and our work together. We were taken back to Wulugu Senior High, and walked to the unveiling of Karimu's memorial plaque. Some of his family were there, including a wife and, importantly, his daughter Sarah. She had been with us on my first stay at Wulugusec, so we sang the *Madam Lynne* song that I remembered from that visit, when the whole school sang with such enthusiasm and joy. As we reached the village a motorbike pulled up in front of us with a cameraman perched precariously on the back. He was from Ghana TV sent to film the celebrations, and we were filmed being greeted by the Chief of Wulugu. Some of the older boys were 'on guard', proudly carrying model rifles. The school had organized a packed programme with speeches, singing, dancing and presentations of gifts. I was surprised to receive new leather cushions, effectively my new throne, bearing my name, Neesim Poanaba, from our dear friend Professor Chief Nabila who first enskinned me 20 years earlier. Then there was the gift of a framed citation from the King of Mamprugu.

ON NEESIM POANABA LYNNE MARY SYMONDS.

From The King and Over-lord of the Mamprugu Kingdom

NAA ABDULAI MAHAMI BUAHAGU SHERIGA 2nd

Today marks a huge milestone in the journey that began 20 years ago. It is a day when we see visibly before our eyes the fruits of your hard work over the years. Wulugu Project, through your unwavering determination to see development and growth of education in Northern Ghana, has affected the lives of countless children, particularly girls. You have produced female medical doctors, so many nurses, teachers, dressmakers, and caterers among others through the numerous schools and vocational schools you have built over the years. Mamprugu and the Kingdoms of Northern Ghana stand today to celebrate your triumph and success and are proud of you in the execution of your duties as Neesim Poanaba. This citation is not a farewell but a pat on the back for being there for your people. You have rescued so many girls from poverty, slavery and early marriages. You will always be the voice of those silenced and the strength of so many weak ones. We congratulate you on your twentieth Anniversary and wish you a long life, good health and strength. The Nayiri and all the people of the Mamprugu Kingdom say:

TI PUSIYA PAM

Thank you very much

At the end of the ceremony I was asked to unveil Karimu's plaque, even though I felt that I was intruding. Then two girls shyly came to me with a little plastic pot labelled 'from WTVS (Walewale Technical and Vocational School). Inside the pot were two necklaces and bracelets that they had made for me. It was one of the most precious gifts I have ever received. So many old friends had come to the durbar, it was hard to find space to talk to them all. The party moved back to Walewale for food prepared by an ex-student at her restaurant, 'Swanky Sparkles'. As we climbed wearily into our truck for the journey back to Tamale, another car screeched in front of us: Ghana radio wanting an interview.

In my own speech I thanked everyone for their part in improving education across the North, congratulating them for the massive shift in attitude towards educating girls. It was is clear that selling daughters into early marriage has become much less common, and the trend now is to encourage girls to move from primary to secondary education, helping them gain the qualifications needed for a career. In the media reports following this, the headline was often the fact that I talked about the damage caused in many countries in allowing university courses that could lead no-where, stressing that apprenticeships and vocational and technical training should be prioritised. Interestingly, similar remarks began to be made in the UK a year later. As this attitude escalated and deepened, it was clearly worrying for those universities offering qualifications that are of little value. The importance of our vocational schools was clear.

***

In 2019, after many years of discontent, Regional Boundaries were re-drawn in Ghana. For the North, this meant that the regions were related to their tribes, and not those decided on by a well-meaning post-colonial administrator. The peoples hope that this will bring an end to the crippling tribal disputes and chieftaincy clashes that the uninformed boundaries have caused.

For 'The Wulugu Project' this means that our 'Northern Region, by far the largest region, has been divided into three. These are: 'North', 'North East' and 'Savannah'

The regions have been carved along tribal lines with each region and its Overlord independently manning the affairs of people.

The majority tribe in the Northern Region is Dagomba. Mamprusi have the North East. Gonja have the large Savanah Region.

These are the majority tribes with their overlords in charge of the geographical areas. It is considered incontestable as they are duly recognized by the minority tribes within the various regions as the custodians of the land. The hope is that will promote the development that is key to defeating the devastating impact of neglect and poverty.

Somehow, over the years, I have been honoured with Chieftaincies of each of these three tribes!

There have been many other honours along the way, none so great as these, although my Honorary Fellowship of the University of Sunderland comes close. The importance of awards is the recognition they give to the many amazing volunteers in Ghana and UK. Most have come 'out of the blue'.

For example, One Sunday afternoon in 2015 there was a call from the U.K. Prime Minister's office in Downing Street. I thought this was a hoax so hung up. But they had searched for a charity that was doing good work to help disadvantaged girls and women, and had chosen the Wulugu Project. This was to coincide with Michelle Obama's visit to the UK to discuss how the difficulties facing girls could be addressed. Michelle was the wife of the USA President. It brought a 'Points of Light' certificate and a letter from Prime Minister David Cameron.

Our work to tackle slavery has continued. In the beginning it was almost a side-effect of our projects, but became increasingly recognised as integral to poverty alleviation. Karimu Nachina summed this up in a letter in 2013:

POSTSCRIPT

Modern Slavery…
…is summed up in this letter from Karimu dated 23rd March 2013

Dear Poanaba/Ewurche,

Modern Slavery can be seen in child trafficking, child labour and the actual trading of children by poor parents. Ghana is noted as a high slavery country in West Africa. It is very difficult to point out cases of modern slavery and trafficking because those who do it have very complicated and sophisticated ways of operating. Illiteracy and poverty are the major cause of people sending their children into slavery. Illiterates tend to marry many wives and have multiple children who are not sent to school. And children who are not in school are good fodder for slavery. They tend to be attracted to people who entice them to follow them to the urban areas for better jobs. Extended family systems have broken down, when every child was taken care of, even if the parents were poor. But now such systems have disintegrated. The land has become impoverished and cannot now support enough food crops to take care of the family. The tendency is for parents to give their children to people in urban areas for meagre sums of money. Even those who are not sold go to the urban areas on their own and end up in the hands of wealthy people who use them and only feed them. There are several examples where trucks have been stationed in villages to collect young girls from the North to take to the South to be used as house helps and maids. Sometimes, some of these maids, after having stayed a long time with their masters or mistresses are given attractive gifts to send back to the village to entice new children for trafficking. The boys are kept home to continue helping on the land and the girls are forced to go to the urban areas to bring extra income home. They fall prey to abuse, exploitation and prostitution. There is a huge economic and social gap between the rural and urban areas and the urban areas remain an attraction for rural children. This has resulted in thousands of girls migrating from rural North to urban South to act as head porters, maidservants and some are actually sold. Some of them are denied the chance of ever visiting their parents. There is a recent example where a girl had to run away from an uncle in the South to the North. She couldn't remember the name of her village and the uncle and the wife would not tell her. She ran away from them in an effort to trace the parents, was involved in an accident and had her left hand amputated at the Tamale Teaching Hospital. Efforts are still being made to help trace her parents. Since Wulugu Project's Intervention opportunities have been opened up for children to go to school, as children not in school form the bulk of children trafficked. Wulugu's seven vocational schools have helped greatly in reducing the number of girls that go to the urban areas. Parents have actually gone to the South to bring back their children to attend these vocational schools. There is pressure for much more help. We just need more funding.

Thank you and God bless you.
Karimu Nachina

Year by year, the transformation of lives continues, now with Solomon, Karimu's eldest son, at the helm. Somewhere there is a right path for those peoples who have been so forgotten. I hope that our role has been to help communities look at what they really need, and to avoid some of the devastating mistakes that are being made across the 'more developed' world. Perhaps, one day, attitudes to donor funding may change. This could result in those NGOs like ours, who have such a cast iron track record, actually having access to the funding they need.

It is important to realise that we aim to enable gentle, careful, truly beneficial change that deals with some of the tragedies of poverty without too much damage to the joyous realities of village life. This is our never-ending story that will eventually continue without our involvement. It is clear that most funders will not believe that a charity without paid staff, publicity machines, large cars and offices and celebrity endorsement can be worthy of their support. We hope that there will be, at some stage, a 'light-bulb moment' that will result in our Ghana team gaining the funding they deserve and would spend so very well. Perhaps someone, somewhere, will read our simple book and respond to it.

Acknowledgements

It is, of course, impossible to recognise individually the hundreds in Ghana and the UK who have, through their faith in the Wulugu Project, together with care, support, strength and wisdom, made dreams of better lives a reality for so many neglected communities. My wish for you all—and you know who you are—is that you feel as proud of yourselves as I feel privileged that our paths have run as one for even a short time. For some of you, your staying power has been incredible. This is what has buoyed me up through the toughest of hours and added to my delight in the many times of triumph. Some of you may have helped only for moments, but those moments were and are an important part of the complex dynamic of change for the better. We have learned so much together in honest partnership and have shown that the 'Wulugu effect' works without need for kudos, celebrity or vast income. Well done to you all, but particularly to those living in the difficult conditions of Northern Ghana that have been your own legacy. You have played a vital role in making things better for your children and your children's children. We in the UK envy the joy of life that shines through your problems.

My husband Roger has been incredible. Both in the UK and in Ghana. In Ghana he has steered me through many challenging days, travelling from village to village, reminding me why we are there, who I am meeting, what we have done and what we need the community to do. And refusing to let me be tired, unwell, or angry. Now that's a husband!

He and the wonderful Joseph Karimu Nachina developed a deep friendship and mutual respect. Karimu is already a legend in Northern Ghana. The results of his selfless work to transform so many lives will live on for generations. Thank you dear Karimu.

Finally, these recollections could not have been brought into print without my editor, Jan Wolf who brought some order out of chaos and constantly encouraged me.